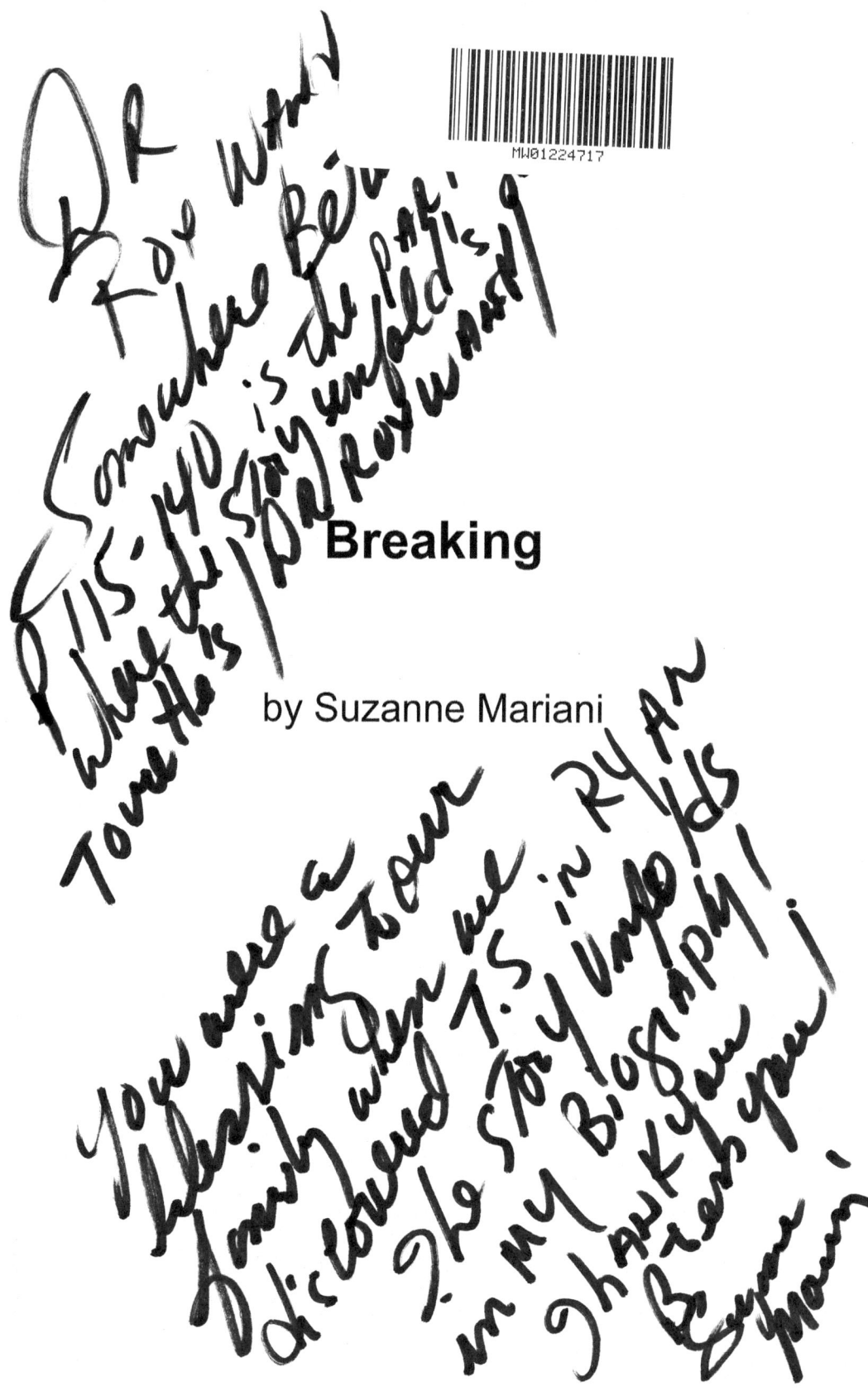

Breaking

by Suzanne Mariani

FriesenPress

Suite 300 - 990 Fort St
Victoria, BC, V8V 3K2
Canada

www.friesenpress.com

Copyright © 2017 by Suzanne Mariani
First Edition — 2017

Editing and Pre-Press
a branch of One Thousand Trees
www.onethousandtrees.com

ISBN
978-1-5255-1864-5 (Hardcover)
978-1-5255-1865-2 (Paperback)
978-1-5255-1866-9 (eBook)

1. BODY, MIND & SPIRIT, INSPIRATION & PERSONAL GROWTH

Distributed to the trade by The Ingram Book Company

Contents

Acknowledgements

First and foremost, enormous gratitude to Donna, Viktoria and Vetta, for letting me burn your ears with endless reading when I needed a straightforward opinion. Your "say-so's" have meant everything to me while writing this book. There is a rule of three, a triad, a three chord song, and three amigos. You have been my "go-to" for the two years I've dedicated myself to writing, and none of you have failed to do anything but support.

Thank you my three beautiful friends who know how to say "That was a dumb idea" just as much as "That was genius!"

I would like to express my gratitude to Michael Kendrick and Ron Lamoureux. To you Michael, for the years of service as my on-call "IT guy" – the forensics of computers. Thank you for prioritizing my book project like your own. Ron, you've helped to create an amazing site and photography for the book launch. Thank you for your patience with me, when I became the "Suzanne on demand."

A shout-out to you both!

A particular thanks to Doug When I met you, it was approximately eight years ago when my band was playing at a venue you were hired to renovate. You loved the music we performed and have never missed a show since. You truly have been my No.1 Fan. Since then, I've hired you for many of my home chores and renos, and the work you do for me is always over and above, especially during the trying times when I was writing this book.

You have helped me so much that I don't want to think how it would have been had I not met you. Thank you!

To Jeff, for your amazing graphics that helped to create words and pictures of my expressions on a canvas that was once blank and without color.

Much obliged!

Owner & Publisher, One Thousand Trees – I owe an Immeasurable appreciation to Lisa Browning. You had the experience, knowledge and the *savoir faire* from the onset. Something I could not have accomplished without your savvy. You've been fabulous from the initial phone call, to editing, and to the launch of the book.

You're a five-star!

Last but not least, a "hat tip" to the colleagues in my office. I see the wind in your sail every day as you whisk by my open door. I love your energy and high-performance attitude. It reminds me of the purpose of making things happen, and it is true that we can do all things.

I am also grateful for many of your friendships!

Dedication

This book is dedicated to my four children, Chantal, Ryan, and the twins, Felice and Anthony. Without you in my life I could not conjure up my true purpose. You are all full of life, ambition and direction. Something I cannot take full credit for, as you all have tenacity in your own wisdom. Yet I know the stars, and how they line up in a design of perfect alignment and beauty. You were born to be perfect, untainted, unblemished and spotless gifts in my eyes and in the core of my heart. As your mother, I know I have disappointed you many times, and this with much regret. So many missed opportunities to praise and build your spirits up. For this I am truly sorry.

For now, my arms are strong, full of energy and steady hands to prepare birthday, Christmas, and Thanksgiving dinners. The quality of life can offer many years, yet the day will come when I will be subdued and be of old age. Your strength will grow and mine will become weak and fragile. If there be nothing left but a breath in me, I will take with me your names that were scripted in my womb and love you without end.

Thank you for the joy you put in my life.

I love you,

Preface

The recollection of a two year old girl's first memory that will take you on a journey of love, hate, fear, passion, anger, failure, rejection and shame. YET, the windows of success, joy, laughter and brief moments of freedom pass through the storm until the "BREAKING"

When you face the end of yourself...

I called this book *Breaking* because that's what it's about. Breaking patterns, breaking depression, breaking any challenge that you might have in your life. I wrote the book based on some of the events of my life, believing it could become a self-help manual for those who might need it.

One of my challenges, at least in the beginning, was to confront my phobia of not being able to leave the house, of not being able to work, of suffering depression, anxiety and panic attacks. Our society doesn't always provide the tools to help people who are faced with these challenges and are not able to take a step forward. I've been fortunate enough to push myself through all of these obstacles in my life without being a victim, without blaming my parents or the world, without proclaiming that nobody loves me or cares about me, that nobody is listening to me, and that I wasn't treated fairly.

Reading my book will take you to a place where you start thinking about who you are in a different way. You may start thinking about what other people go through and suddenly find yourself wanting to give to other people because it takes the focus off what you're going through. It will change the whole pattern of the energy in and around you.

In the end, *Breaking* not only is an *autobiography*, but also a self-help book based on events that have taken place in my life, with a little bit of personal advice on how to get through some of those challenges. I'm hoping the book will help all those who need to forgive themselves, to believe that there is another day and that they can breathe again.

BREAKING

1

Flashback

It's 1961, I'm just two years old, and my parents of French origin have just settled into a turn-of-the century home in Winnipeg, Manitoba. From a little girl's perspective, there was nothing unusual about the environment surrounding me. Like most children growing up, having fun was my main focus. I have many fond memories of playing with neighborhood kids on the street all summer long during school holidays.

Little did I know that those memories would become the peak of painful reflections in my life for many years.

Had I known then what I know now, I would have desperately wanted to avoid the painful, devastating life that awaited me. At that time, we had neighbors all around us with lots of children. And though there were many families in the area, there's one family I will never forget: the Lamoix family.

Mr and Mrs Lamoix and their 15 children lived in a small two-storey home that was almost 1300 square feet in size. I remember having a crush on almost all the Lamoix boys. I had a dream that one of them would be my Superman, and rescue me some day.

The question is, rescue me from what?

Even at a young age, it seemed that my dreams were prophesying my future. Night after night I would have in my sleep, a flash visualization of being saved from a world that was about to devour me. I didn't realize that God was preparing me for a life that would be filled with trauma and many adversarial challenges.

Growing up, I never received any positive affirmation from my parents. Both felt that good parenting consisted of putting a roof over our heads and food on the table. There was an unspoken rule that we weren't to talk back – a rule that took precedence in our home at all times.

If we got out of line, we paid for it. I remember my mother hitting me so hard with a belt that it drew blood. On one instance she went out of control with her spanking and it left me lying exhausted on the cold laminate floor. That day concluded with beauty for ashes as my mother became extremely compassionate and remorseful for her actions. Hugs and warm kisses! Something strange to me, yet I embraced those new warm feelings of comfort and safety.

While I felt violated by spankings with a spoon, belt or hand, it was on an emotional level worse for me to watch my parents punish my brothers. I watched my dad grab them with one arm, and then swing the belt with the other.

My brothers would dance madly around in an effort to get away from the whipping that would be inflicted by that strap. (As I did.)

To this day, it's a memory that's hard to erase. I realize now hitting us hard and talking down to us at times was a method of trying to keep us humble – especially me, as I was a very expressive child.

Laughter was rare in our household, but when it happened, it was genuine. If there was affection or love, it was an unfamiliar sensation because it was so rare to experience those emotions. Yet, there was laughter, and fun, when we played board games, told jokes or played hide-and-seek.

However, that harmony was usually short-lived. Someone would eventually lose their temper, or a disagreement would break out, putting us in a war zone once again. That zone was filled with hair pulling, punching, hitting and kicking. We often left the scene with the other sibling crying. No one ever said "Sorry."

However, my brother Paul was different. For the most part, our relationship was harmonious. He had a stuttering problem (which he triumphantly overcame in later years), but it never seemed to affect his self-esteem, even though he was teased often by kids at school, and his siblings.

Paul and I were similar in that we showed more emotion, and as a result, we were labeled as being "over-sensitive." Our shared trait, it turns out, actually acted as a safekeeping trait that bound us together in a close relationship that we still hold dearly today.

I recall a time when Paul cut his foot on a piece of glass, and ended up in a wheelchair for several weeks. The doctor didn't want him to put any pressure on it, as the nerve had nearly been severed. We were told that he could possibly end up with a paralyzed foot if it didn't heal properly.

Well, that didn't stop my mischievous younger brother (Alain) from trying to have some "fun" with Paul.

One day, he suggested that it was a perfect, sunny day for a stroll. He told Paul that he'd be happy to take him for a peaceful outing in the afternoon sun. Blissfully ignorant, Paul accepted gratefully, having no idea of what was lurking around the corner for him, or in this case, down a steep hill.

As Paul described it, it was an interesting excursion to say the least. Once they reached the top of the hill, Alain decided to let the wheelchair go. With fascination, he watched it glide faster and faster, reaching the bottom of the hill at a crazy speed.

Predictably, the wheel chair tumbled over, throwing a screaming, sobbing Paul, who justifiably was fearful for his life. Paul later said that he couldn't believe that his own flesh and blood could take such pleasure in betraying and abandoning him.

Over the years, such experiences with his brother were frequent. Bit by bit, Paul's trust in his brother disappeared, and there were no kind words between them as Paul's mood escalated into bitterness. As the years passed, I would join Paul in a life journey that was characterized by negativity and a jumble of unresolved emotions.

2

Family

Sitting around the kitchen table at supper one night, everyone was present except for my parents; they had gone away on holidays and left us with a passive aunty and a bullying uncle.

Although I can't recall where they went on their vacation, I certainly recall the hollowness I felt being left with these relatives, who were acting as our temporary guardians.

The ambiance of my house changed. It was like walking into an unfurnished room that was vacant of any affection whatsoever. The atmosphere caused an immediate heaviness of heart.

My uncle, the "man of no inhibitions," was always ready to give us a good back hand if we were disobedient, as he was instructed by my parents to do so at his discretion. Like a ritualistic morning prayer, he would remind us daily of that until the day my parents returned. When we were out of line he did things like make us kneel against the wall with our arms up. Another incident that comes to mind is when he demanded my brother to eat a particular food that would make him gag.

When we were left to be watched by someone (whether babysitter or guardian) their behavioral management seemed very much like that of my parents.

My father, being a passive personality, followed my mother's instructions to essentially spank us on her demand. It was no surprise to see this reserved and soundless man, who continually submitted to any authoritative voice, become a non-communicating alcoholic.

I remember watching my father, his eyes red and breath tinged with the smell of booze, sitting at the kitchen table trying to eat dinner one early evening. Predictably, he missed his mouth as he tried to balance food on his fork. Inevitably, it ended up scattering, some on his plate, some on ours, and some on the floor.

A head cook in a seniors' home, he'd started there at the age of fourteen. As things turned out, it was the only job he ever knew. He never took on any hobbies, and his life was, to his detriment, consumed by work, drinking, puttering, and sleeping his binges off on the couch.

To his credit, however, he was a very active man in his younger days. Before the drinking took over, he was a handyman around the house, performing renovations or tinkering around in the garage. He rarely spoke and was considered by others to be extremely shy and introverted. He would never say no if you required help.

His soft heart became hardened over the years by people who took advantage of his warm and passive nature. A man who was once gentle, quiet and warm-hearted became increasingly withdrawn. His pent-up anger often came to the surface when he spanked us on what seemed to be a violent impulse that came from out of nowhere.

He would justify that violent impulse as a bona-fide (sincere) punishment – a spanking (buckle of the belt) that turned the warm tones of the young pink skin on our thighs, legs, and arms a horrible mottled black and blue.

Ultimately, he died of an aneurysm at the young age of sixty-four. He was a sullen man who was in denial about his alcoholism, and left this world bitter.

– Back to the home front –

A front that was chilling to the bone emotionally! I dreaded to hear my parents say "bed time," as this meant lights out, and to be locked down in the dark. I was never prepared but did expect the same familiar demons to visit me on the clock, and they would never cease to be late.

Still under ten years old, I'd be haunted by a cascade of creepy sounds that funneled through the old house. All the strange, blood-curdling events that accompanied those sounds robbed me of what should have been carefree and joyful years. My early years were marked by a disorienting whirlwind of chronic anxiety, fear and uncontrollable panic attacks.

By the age of 13 I could not escape the idea that my house was possibly haunted. I remember screaming at the top of my lungs as I felt snakes crawling all over me while lying in my bed. My mother, who hated to be awakened, ran into the room trying desperately to calm me down. All her attempts of reasoning failed and she ultimately grabbed my hand and forced it upon the bed where I was watching with my own eyes snakes slithering and squirming over each other and their legions of many covered my bed like a blanket.

With great fear I watched as my hand was forced down to touch the snakes on my bed and when it did the image completely disappeared.

Within a year of that eerie episode I found myself in the midst of another supernatural mystery. I was just about to fall into a deep sleep when a sudden movement of my blanket alerted me. I could feel at the corner of my bed that someone was pulling the blanket down, and I thought perhaps it was one of my brothers playing a game. I quickly grabbed the blanket back and pulled it in towards me. It pulled back at the other end abruptly and it became a tug of war.

It was dark in the room and I couldn't see well enough who could possibly be pulling with such authoritative force. Until...

The blanket jolted up in the air in an elevated state and there was no one holding it up. I screamed, let go of the blanket, and ran out into the living room. I jumped over the coffee table and onto the lap of my mother. In a panic state and mumbling in French, "J'ai peur, aide moi!" (I'm afraid help me!) I remember my father in his shocked state commented on my hair as it was standing up on end. I had a short pixy cut and not one hair on my head was limp or flexible.

Several months later I heard my father share a chilling story of our home. He explained that he was in the basement late one evening, and heard us kids running around upstairs, laughing and playing. He was angry and made his way up in a hurry to scold us and put us back to bed. When he arrived to the top of the stairs all was quiet. He knew we would not have had time to jump back into our beds, and was horrified by this spine-chilling occurrence when he realized we were all sound asleep.

3

Kindred

When I was approximately nine or ten, my parents separated us and I now had my own bedroom on the main floor. (Finally!) My three brothers were moved to the basement, where it was very humid and full of creepy crawly silverfish. Over the years my two older brothers never talked much about the strange phenomena in that house. (Perhaps they had no experiences.) In fact I don't remember ever having a conversation with them about it. We were never close. Other than to argue, we never had deep or warm conversations as I did with my baby brother Paul. He and I were connected on so many levels.

Paul struggled more than I did with the supernatural occurrences in that house. He had experiences none of us would ever want to encounter. He claimed that night after night demons (little men) would come out from under his bed and talk with him. (Or as he put it visit with him.) To Paul this was the story of Peter and the wolf.

The little men would call him Peter, and since he was only five or six years old he eventually adjusted to this as being a normal part of life. These experiences led him in later years to a world of drugs, alcohol, and primarily cocaine. He had to cope with life's secret challenges, which he could tell no one about.

Paul was the one I clung to for brotherly support. However, he would set my emotional compass off the chart when he shared his spiritual experiences with me. He claimed our mother repeatedly ignored his crying and fears when it was time for bed. In her justifiable defense, she was unable to understand the information he was trying to articulate to her. Crying or not, it was off to bed! Paul eventually gave up the effort, and accepted the fact that nothing was going to change.

He would converse with the little men as they crawled out from under his bed to engage with him almost every night. Paul's description was that they were extraterrestrial beings. He became comfortable with them.

It seemed as if these experiences were isolated to a few of us in the home, including a renter who lived upstairs. She too complained on occasion of her own eerie experiences.

Paul had a bad set of cards dealt to him. He experienced a deep level of spiritual confusion that did not seem to affect our other two brothers as much. Alain became a Jehovah witness in his search for spiritual conquest. He made this decision just before he ran away from home at the age of seventeen. He clung to it till his death. He had an aneurysm at the age of forty-nine that snatched life from him faster than you can take a breath! (He preceded my father, who died of the same thing.)

The oldest brother was a "matter of fact kind of guy." He was very efficient in doing his own thing, in his own time. He was the type of guy that would sweep anything he considered a nuisance under the rug and would never give it another thought. This was something that didn't come naturally to the rest of us. I believe that could have been a coping mechanism in an unsecure and unstable environment.

He had the guts we lacked, and he always came across as the tough one, who knew how to pull up his socks when it was time to. I was intimidated by him most of the time because he was the one who didn't cry, even when he was hurt.

Love, understanding, compassion and attention were not fundamental emotions within our family.

– Growing up –

It wasn't long before I was thrust into the drama of high school and was introduced to my first boyfriend. Coming from a strong Catholic background, my parents did address the premarital sex thing. I was told going to hell would be the exonerated reward, so I promptly learned to keep my legs crossed.

Catholicism in the 60's and 70's was a serious matter to my grandmother. She had pledged allegiance to it early on as it was, in her mind, the only true religion. I had been admonished by her to never date a black person; after all, it is better for people to be with their own race, she would say. It made sense at the time.

Without ever connecting the dots, this was my first unequivocal introduction to racism.

Since I was sensitive in nature, it was straightforward to me that she was the wise one and I needed an intuitive mentor. (Grandmothers are perfect for that!) She had a style that was powerfully convincing to her audience. Her storytelling was always set up for the stage. She was bold, yet diplomatic; a woman who would appear to have confidence even when she had none. The most profound yet disturbing statement she ever made to me was that anyone outside our Catholic faith would undeniably be tormented with fire and brimstone. Hell and Hades where there is gnashing of teeth. Going to hell in other words, ouch, ouch!

My grandmother (my father's mother) was in my view often a sour and critical woman. She was nonetheless close to her own children (my uncles and aunties), and cared for them deeply. She was traditional with dinner parties and entertained well with her French cuisine dishes. She died at an old age, years later than her husband, my grandfather. He was considered a man of few words and sometimes none. He was very much like his son, my father.

My grandmother had an interesting background, which she said we proudly inherited. It was something my grandmother spoke about very often. It was her "claim to fame" being related to the famous *Dionne family!*

– Tall story –

It is still foggy to her siblings that her family's Quebec roots would inevitably be tied to the history of this family. Was it a myth in the legend of our family roots? It all started with her mother (my great grandmother, Albertine Dionne) who was born in Quebec. It was told Albertine was a cousin to Oliva (father of the famous Dionne quintuplets).

A woman by the name of Elzire Dionne gave birth to five identical quintuplet girls on May 28th, 1934.

In 1935 the provincial government of Canada removed the quintuplets from their parents, as there were no records of anyone having quintuplets worldwide, and so they stepped in to take over the well being of the quintuplets. The government and those around them began to inevitably profit by making the quintuplets a worldwide tourist attraction.

The father Oliva,   signed a contract to exhibit the quintuplets at the World's Fair in Chicago. Although Oliva had remorse the following day and wanted to cancel, the authorities stepped in anyway, claiming they needed to protect the five girls.

The parents lost their rights to any decision-making, as the children became wards of the Provincial Crown.

The quintuplets became Canada's largest attraction. They were used in advertisements, and products such as souvenirs and postcards, which were sold with the Dionne quintuplets' logo. It generated millions of dollars for the province of Ontario, and some say the outpouring of money kept the province from going bankrupt. At that time many Canadian homes owned a quintuplet doll.

Hollywood exploited their fame, and several movies were made by 1939. In 1978 they re-did the story as a television movie, and I watched it with a grieved heart.

The children were raised in a facility with a nine room nursery. It was staffed with many nurses to care for the girls, and several police officers to guard them.

Like a circus show you could pay to view them through a glass window.

The Dionne parents won back custody of their children in 1943; unfortunately it ended with a chilling report that they indubitably were abusive to their beautiful quintuplet girls.

I remember entering the back yard porch of my grandmother as a little girl and seeing the picture of the Dionne family hanging on the wall. She was honored her mother was a "Dionne." With the picture in a frame and no glass, it eventually crumbled.

I loved my grandmother but it wasn't until her passing that I began to unveil why she had at times an ice-cold wintry demeanor.

As a child her mother (Albertine Dionne) died shortly after giving birth to one of her brothers, leaving her father to raise her and her four siblings alone.

Unfortunately he was unable to care for them properly and temporarily placed them in two independent orphanages. The children were afraid, and emotionally traumatized by this separation.

My grandmother shared on many occasions how she was abused both verbally and physically in the orphanage. I can only imagine the grief she and her siblings felt losing their mother and then having to deal with the destructive emotion of abandonment from their father, who inevitably ended up an alcoholic.

My grandmother's baby sister Simone was five at the time, and due to the trauma she became a chronic bed-wetter. With no mother and being removed from her father, all she had to cling to for love was my grandmother, her big sister.

From the age of five to seven the orphanage workers would take the wet and urinated sheets from Simone's bed and place them over her head during the day in a public place, in order to embarrass and humiliate her never to wet the bed again. Unfortunately the stress and demand was not a successful disciplinary action, and it was told that, at the young age of seven, Simone died of a broken heart.

Simone also suffered from a disease called Danse De St. Guy, or the English version St. Vitus dance disease. Similarly

Sydenham Chorea which is a neurological disorder of childhood, which could have possibly been the related ailment.

It is an infection caused by Group A beta-hemolytic strepto-coccus. This is the same bacterium responsible for causing acute rheumatic fever which was not uncommon then. St. Vitus dance disease is considered a movement disorder having traits of involuntary movements and /or tics.

There is a legend of an Italian martyr from Sicily, named Vitus. He had delivered the emperor's daughter of an evil spirit. It is believed he lived during the reign of the Roman emperor Diocletian around 303 A.D. Because he was a Christian, he was subjected to many tortures. He died as a martyr during the persecution of Christians and was soon named Saint Vitus.

Perhaps things were not so bad in my world, compared to this!

Although there was little demonstration of affection with any parent or grandparent, I still had a sense of belonging. I had a school to go to, a house to live in, and …. Nothing else I can think of. I was empty, lonely, deserted and most often felt apart from everyone. I was the outcast who could never fit in anywhere. Inside I could feel the warmth of my own heart, the desire to be good, to love, and to be loved. A passion was living in me but I had no one to guide me. I was alive but I was dead!

This departure of emotion put me in the accompaniment of a phenomenon called Astral Projection, where my conscious mind left my physical body. I remember going to bed one night feeling numb and without concern of anything. The sensation of leaving my body was as though I was allowing myself to die. Completely relaxed and almost asleep, it was as if I was going to run away somewhere, but I didn't know where.

Like a child leaving the womb of a mother through the birth canal, so it was as my inner spirit began to slip out of my body. The jolt was but a moment when I caught myself like the lifeline of a rope and pulled myself back into my body. This abnormal event never took place in my life again. Thank Goodness!

With all these detached emotions I longed for something to feel right. Instead, I was a magnet to failure, with no acceptance from anyone. I thought maybe I could dye my hair to look prettier, but my mother said that was only for pretty girls to do. That comment stayed with me for what felt like a lifetime. This is not what mothers say to their daughters. She had been abused herself growing up, mostly by her father. Belt spankings were a form of punishment well accepted in that era in many homes. She too had little affection, and understanding was not acknowledged as a form of communication in her household. She said many things to me out of anger, things that took my heart years to erase.

She never had good eyesight and would bump into things for many years as a child, before getting her own pair of glasses. She also had a stuttering problem, and was maliciously teased by other school children. Being left-handed naturally, she was forced to write with her right hand and was severely disciplined if she was caught making a switch of hands.

With little education, she had to fight to be noticed, and to survive in a world where she herself was not held in high esteem.

But even so, forgiveness was something that took me a lifetime to hand over to her. It was me that needed to understand.

Her buffeting me came naturally and habitually to her. Wounds, abuse and rejection were all she knew. She was in her own ignorance, blindly passing the baton. Somehow over time, together in agreement, we brought that thing to its knees and we were both set free!

———————⊃●⊂———————

4

Rewind

Backtracking to the memories of my elementary and high school days is a boisterous reflection, to say the least. Flashbacks are easy triggers to go to when certain circumstances seem justifiably merited. I used to wonder, "Why did that person react when I said this or that?" when I myself was the queen of this boomerang reaction to others.

It's easy to watch someone else react hostilely and question it, but we never see ourselves in that mirror. —SM

At least that's how it was for me, ignorant to understanding my own behaviors but quick to judge everyone else's.

This problem was not easy to fix. The word communication was dormant in me and I did not comprehend the process of how it worked. I was trapped inside, with no stable anchor of understanding, and therefore failed miserably in this area of my life. These feelings of being unwanted at home cleared a path for me to search for acceptance somewhere else. If I had to backtrack to where it started, I would say grade one would be the starting point. Thirty students in a classroom is no picnic when everyone is hastily sparring to belong to the coolest and most popular clique.

The school was run by The Grey Nuns Organization. (Les Soeurs Grises). They wore black hobbits which muddled me and so I dared to ask "Why are you wearing black hobbits if you call yourselves grey nuns?" (laughing at my own jokes) but the retort was usually a simple but profound brash smirk. They were very conservative in an orthodox style, and it was conclusively unbecoming to say the least.

The school had classes for either all French or all English. (I was all French.)

The unyielding rule in my house was "NO ENGLISH!" (This did not last.) Being very proud of myself for learning my first English word through my peers, I did say to my mother one day, "Je suis tres thirsty" (I am very thirsty). I never forgot the slap on the head for that one!

Although most of the teachers in my elementary school consisted of nuns, there were certainly some who were not. One in particular I will never forget was a large teacher with man hands, man feet and a man's body. Strangely enough she was a woman. She was older in years but that didn't deter us from whispering and name calling behind her back. Because she had such a large face to go with that beefcake, we called her bulldog big foot! It is not something I'm proud of, but it seemed funny at the time.

Teachers hitting children was the "norm" in this elementary school, so it seemed. The majority of us did get slapped when we were out of line. I remember one time watching a teacher grab the ears of one of my classmates, then try to lift him from the ground.

– Temporary insanity –

My grade one teacher, whom I had the pleasure to have for two years, did fail me of her own accord.

The disturbing memory of her locking me in her classroom closet still materializes within me every time I take an elevator, or if I am in an enclosed area. I've had to fight claustrophobia most of my life due to that incident. I practiced going up and down elevators over time without telling anyone how fearful this was for me. For years I would take the option of climbing the stairs as an alternative, to cover up my trepidation, anxiety and insecurity. It was all caused by that one traumatic event. To this day I still remain in conflict as to what I did wrong to receive such a disturbing punishment from my grade one teacher. But I do remember the resounding shriek of my own voice as I screamed with great fear, in the hopes of someone letting me out.

I was only seven years old. Who would not be afraid of the dark, being forced in a room not wider that four feet, from which is no escape other than by the one who holds the key? I was panic-stricken and perplexed. Although the students could hear me scream in terror, none would dare to leave their seat. I remember some of the students had watery eyes when I was finally let out.

Students were ruled with the iron fist, and warned that this could happen to them if they didn't listen. By the time I was let out of the teacher's coat closet my eyes were fiery red and swollen. I was unable to catch my breath for several minutes with all the uncontrollable sobbing. I spoke to no one that day; my heart was shattered.

Times were sure different then they are today, after the evolving years in education, curricula, rules and policies. Teachers had authority to be substitute parents when it came to discipline, and pretty much everything was allowed for punishment, or so it seemed. Parents believing hearsay of teachers, and not their own children, was often and unfortunately advocated in this school.

I experienced teachers hitting, slapping, and even kicking, mostly the boys.

This takes me back to a time in grade four where I had a serious injury from falling off a teeter totter during a fifteen minute school recess.

One of the teachers brought me in to see the principal to discuss my injury. I was still in shock and therefore did not feel the pain of what turned out to be a broken bone. I felt dizzy and wanted to faint. Unfortunately, that did not deter the nun in the hobbit (principal) to assume the responsibility of getting me any medical attention. She simply sent me home, and I walked a mile by myself

Fortunately, my mother, who happened to have the day off from work, was home. She immediately called my father, and arrangements were made to take me to the hospital, and there I received my first cast. I give credit to my mother, who I remember was not happy with the school for sending me to walk home alone in such a vulnerable state.

5

Moments

I never talked to myself as a child, and I don't think there was really any "thinking" going on. It was more knee jerk reactions and emotional wind ups.

As a result I did not do well in school. I probably was capable but I was unable to concentrate and felt powerless. Part of the battle was dealing with my days of being a little girl but not living like one.

Lying on a cold linoleum floor in front of my parents' bedroom door in the middle of the night was where the shifting of my heart occurred, and where I lost that little girl.

Under nine years old with an unyielding nightmare in my head, I ran for safety to the arms of my parents to feel secure and protected. Their bedroom door was locked and I could not enter. They were sound asleep and my mouth was fixed shut.

Being prohibited to wake them was a rule that was rarely broken. In my mind, the thought of being ushered back to my bed with a fuming angry parent would be more tormenting to deal with. Hours went by in the dark of the night as I lay on a cold chilly floor. Quiet as a mouse, if I could just wedge my little fingers through the narrow space under the door, then I could comfort myself and feel like I was snuggled between them.

I believed peace, quietness, and enviable security lay on the other side, where blankets of love and warmth resided. The reality was that even in the torment of fear I lay in my pool of tears till dawn and never made a sound.

Psalm 73:25 in the Old Testament is a transcribed word from King David that reads, "Who have I in Heaven but you?" He cries out to the only one (God) who will answer and never forsake him.

All I knew was, "Who do I have on this earth to depend on but you, my parents?".

This too shall pass, and so it did! The teenage years were around the corner and I was on a journey of music consumption with all the latest radio hits. Every day after school I danced in my room to all the songs and learned all their lyrics. I wasn't a singer as I was horribly off key, but that did not deter me.

I was the little princess who would get a prince one day. I would be on the platform with thousands in front of me as they all applauded my angelic singing voice on the big stage. I was a dreamer for sure! I had visions of having it all!

These moments were mere pockets of escape. For me, daydreaming was a prodigious pastime. I would take the empty cup of my soul and fill it with "Clouds of Wonder!" Unfortunately a "dream bubble" usually comes to a bursting point, so when the music stopped, so did I.

Lalita Tademy, the New York Times bestselling author of three historical novels, once said- "One thing for sure, life goes on with or without you."

A very powerful statement that can also suggest, "So why bother?"

It has taken me many years to overcome the negative thought that I am incapable of reaching any of my dreams. I have learned through a very painful and disheveled journey that "on purpose thinking" is the key to stay focused, and to continue to be vigilant in my thoughts.

I can be more than what I see in myself today. —SM

Agoraphobia, clinical depressions, broken marriages, and even dealing with an exorcism are but a few challenges I contended with. With no one guiding me about straightforward distinctions between the obvious right and wrong thinking, I often fell back in the old pattern of never reviewing my thoughts. I just knew that when I finally dealt with one storm in my life another one would be right behind, waiting to make its grand entrance.

6

Jump

Whenever I think back to my teenage years, I get a captivating memory that had imprisoned my mind for many years. My boyfriend of grade eight, whom I experienced as my first love and first kiss, was about to fragmentize, and impair an already crumbled heart.

It happened at an afternoon party, that ended up with my boyfriend and his friends dragging me down to the basement after everyone else left. There were four or five of them, and I will never forget the sound of my own screams as they pinned me down on the cold cement floor and inappropriately touched me. The violation, the feeling of being restrained forcibly, was an unbearable five minutes of my life.

Hoping my boyfriend's mother would be arriving home at any time, I continued hollering out her name. I could not think of anything else to do as I had been subdued and there was no escape. My voice and her name was my only sword. They finally let me go, and I rushed up those stairs and out of that house faster than I ever thought my adrenalin would take me.

It was a long walk home with a cocktail of intoxicating emotions running through my mind.

I didn't know to cry, be sad, or angry. My thoughts were muddled as my heart raced to register "What just happened to me?" Was this a rape? What was different in their actions other than they didn't follow through to the finish line? I had been fighting for my life till I was exhausted. Since I was not very good at articulating or breaking things down to a point of understanding, I chose to ignore what had happened. I pushed it down low and deep, making sure it could never resurrect again. The conflicting feelings of shame and even guilt overwhelmed me, knowing I had to face them again at school the next day. It was a hornet's nest of humiliation and disgrace.

It wasn't my fault, but there was no support from the voice in my head that was trying to tell me otherwise. And so I lived in the denial of that incident for many years.

I became very good at pretending nothing was wrong, and quickly learned the skills to survive, and to be tough in life rather than curl up and die. Having said that, I certainly have had my share of many long cries from other wounds, followed by my shaking the dust off my feet to get myself back up again.

At the age of sixteen I met a very charismatic and clean-cut guy. He was eighteen years old, with blond hair, and a solid body shape. He was not short of girls being attracted to him. He was a French singer around town, and came from a very large family. He was employed with a fur company where he worked overtime during the week, and so I saw him very little.

He managed to slip away every Tuesday night at six o'clock, where we met at a ten-pin bowling alley to play with the team of our league.

I had never competed in any tournament, as the registration was always more than I could afford. I ended the season with 175 bowling average, which at that time would have qualified me to join professional tournaments.

It was all short-lived when we started our second season. I was not feeling well one evening, and asked my boyfriend to find someone to take my place on the team. There had been this attractive forty-year-old woman who was sparing for the league, and inevitably she was my spare that night.

The arrangement was that my boyfriend would come over to have hot tea with me after the team was done playing, something he and I did together in a quaint little corner of the house, where we would just sit and talk for hours. But this night he never showed up. With many phone call attempts, his mother invariably repeated the same thing with each call. "He simply is not home."

Since he was working overtime the rest of the week we did not have much time to communicate on the phone. I had to wait till the weekend to talk about it.

I did not have the backbone of patience as my intuition and internal radar was warning me something was very wrong. I was indubitably restless about approaching the subject.

We finally had our moment and our tea. I wondered how long it was going to take him to bring it up, but he never did. Eventually we ended up in my parents' back yard, where he was kicking a ball around with one of my brothers. He came over, sat beside me and began to weep. He had been holding in his heart a package of self-condemnation. It took a few minutes to collect himself, and then he enduringly regurgitated what he could no longer keep to himself. He had slept with the forty year old woman and was filled with remorse and self-disgust.

We had never been together the way he was with that woman. My strong Catholic background and the voice of my grandmother were still roaring around in my head about being a virgin until I married. My erroneous guilt for making this moral choice rattled through my mind as those powerful and hurtful words flowed out of his mouth like a sluggish slow-motion picture.

Weeks went by before I could shake off the shock of what had actually taken place. It was even more difficult to cast out the thoughts of their intimate moments together as my imagination played it in rewind over and over in my head. The violation, the humiliation and the shame were ambiguous emotions to grapple with. I was, after all, only sixteen, and the other woman I was contending with was a mature forty.

Once the storm blew over, my boyfriend and I did adjust to that lurid event and managed to put it behind us, somewhat.

Although there were no words spoken about it again, there was a shutdown of some sort, or a growing apart. He strived to meet all my needs, but the distance between us came from me exclusively. Something must have snapped in me when he disclosed his provocative communion with her.

My life was becoming a pocket of secrets I could tell no one. Another violation, another betrayal!!

7

Rearrange

What does a man do when he really wants a woman? He asks for a lifetime commitment. With aloofness between my boyfriend and me, he decided to marry me as a quick-fix solution to the distance between us. Instead of watching me slip through his fingers, he decided to put a ring on one of mine. I don't remember how he proposed, but I must say that I flaunted that ring everywhere. I quit school and went to work full-time. I was getting married; I would be set for life! Or so I thought ...

Wedding plans were in the works, and I had four enthusiastic bridesmaids. Their dresses were charmingly tailored by a seamstress and my fiancé's siblings all pitched in to help with the plans.

Keeping busy in life can allow the flow of "wherever the road takes you" but eventually you will hit a quiet spot where you get to think about where you really want to be. —SM

Is this who I want to wake up to every day for the rest of my life? Am I in love? For me the answer was an echoing "No."

Marrying for security or to avoid loneliness is a big mistake. Some people marry because it's simply a compatible union. It's not about finding the right person but rather becoming the right person. It's taking into consideration "How does this person make me feel when I'm around them?" As I mentioned in the previous chapters, I was a failure in contending with right feelings and emotions.

I suppose I was a bit of a coward. I wasn't brave enough to break it off. I had many people to answer to, and I couldn't bring myself to do it without the perfect situation in place. It's so much easier if you find someone else in the process, isn't it? And that's exactly what happened!

He was in the same group of people we all partied with, and after many conversations I found myself on the phone with him every night. He was the Don Johnson of Miami Vice look-alike, and there wasn't a single girl who wouldn't admit he was worth the chase.

I had butterflies in my stomach, a sensation I never felt before, and it was very euphoric. I was falling in love. He was shy, quiet and reserved. My fiancé was a "boisterous" loud personality and always had to be the center of the party. I think part of the attraction to this new guy was his suave and calm temperament, which was similar to my father's.

I finally drummed up whatever courage I had, and ended the engagement.

It was only weeks before the wedding. My fiancé and I had just purchased a home, and it wasn't a pretty conversation when we tried to get our deposit back.

He was devastated, and I was a wreck myself. My heart was taking me somewhere else, and I could not fight or change the direction my life was now taking me. I didn't love this man anymore, and I knew he could not be trusted. I would catch him flirting with other women in inappropriate ways when he was drinking, and it had soured my stomach too many times.

I remained friends with one of his sisters, Louise, whom I love dearly. We held a very strong relationship then, as we do today, and she was my advocate when it came to his side of the family. Their father was a very big and strong man with the voice of a bear, while their mother was meek and mild. This family had many financial struggles trying to raise twelve children in a very small house. To add to the hardship, one of them was blind.

Laughter was a common thread between them all, and I strongly believe this was the key to the close affection they all had with one another.

Many years went by and they lost their father to an illness. When their mother was on her deathbed at home, I received a call from Louise to stop in to have my last visit with her. I was in my forties at the time. The sisters were gathered around her, but they left the moment I walked in the room. "Take your time with

Mom," they said. This woman made the best homemade buns on the planet, and that's the first thing I reminded her of, and how much I missed them melting in my mouth after coming fresh out of her oven. Glazed with hot butter and topped with a sprinkle of sugar, I recalled. She smiled at me, and with her eyes opening for a grand view of something she whispered, "I love you Suzanne. You are as one of my daughters. I never forgot you!"

She was an amazing woman, and I would have loved to have her as my mother-in-law. But there were no stars lining up for that divine moment, and so it never came to pass.

At the funeral Louise and her husband Jim saw me sitting in the back of the church and they ushered me as I reluctantly followed them to the front with the immediate family. A privilege I did not deserve.

– Looking back –

I was seventeen with the new fine-looking boyfriend. My ex-fiancé was bent upon stalking me somewhat. There were phone calls to me, to my family, and everyone else who would listen to him. He still struggled with the breakup and had a difficult time moving on without me in his life. Although I felt compassion for him I knew his vulnerable state would only get worse if we remained in this steady and unruly communication that seemed to never end.

I had moved out on my own, into a quaint little apartment, and I worked full-time for the Federal Business Development bank. I was the "bubbly" receptionist who loved the meet-and-greet aspect of the job.

I distinctly remember coming home from work one night and my new boyfriend John surprised me at the door with a bag of Chinese take-out food. What a refreshing treat after a long stodgy bus ride from my downtown office. I was completely exhausted. I had very little furniture and just a few dishes with unmatching cutlery. It was very much a barren suite.

Just as we were about to relax for the evening there was a very heavy knock at my apartment door. John offered to see who it was, as I was very complacent and in a laid back mood, having just experienced an incredible foot rub.

Within seconds of John turning the inside latch of the door, there was a resounding thump against the wall, and I thought for sure it was about to crash down or crumble. I had never experienced the earth from underneath me move, but this was an exceptional shock as I was completely unaware as to where it was coming from.

In an unforeseen and abrupt moment John was thrust into my living room with blood gushing out of his nose. And there was my ex-fiancé tumbled over him, all liquored up, savagely kicking and punching him repeatedly. Mathew had so much pent-up anger in him I thought I was witnessing a murder as I watched the blood flowing down John's arm while he was seized in a hitched headlock. Somehow John managed to slip out of that position and flew out the damaged door. I watched as Mathew began to chase him but an impedimentary moment overcame him and everything was at a standstill.

Without any warning I was violently thrown onto a chair where he frantically hovered over me. He was out of control and pacing around me like I was vulnerable prey (which I was). I thought for sure the police would show up any time but the hours went by. He held me hostage in my own apartment, sometimes crying over my lap, and then would flip his personality into another frightening rage. Where were the neighbors? And where was my boyfriend? I was alone and trapped with a very enraged man who was not forgiving of me leaving him.

I was quiet and still like a mouse, the way I was when I lay on the cold linoleum floor when I was afraid I'd wake my parents. My mouth was fixed shut, and Mathew eventually let all his steam out without striking me.

I can only believe that it was by divine intervention that I had not been the one to have opened that door.

———◦———

8

Conflict

This little piggy ran home! John was not the prince I was waiting for, as he left me with a mad man all night while he hightailed it out of there to lick his ego-breaking wounds. However, love does funny things, as at the time all I felt was hurt. I didn't see the truth until I was more mature and became razor-sharp about these types of life experiences.

I had a friend at the time, Michelle, who was from a healthier family … or should I say less dysfunctional. She was my startup kit in getting me to see things the way they really were. I just ran on emotions all the time, with no real training on thinking through any situation without reacting to it first. I came from a family of yellers and screamers (my mother's side). Michelle sat down with me to go over what had just happened. This was something I had never done with anyone before. I recall it was so therapeutic to be in discussion about how to figure things out, to investigate further, to interpret and best of all to sympathize with myself.

At the time I had been diagnosed with an over-reactive thyroid gland which kept me very thin, and I was also undernourished, living on the poverty line trying to sustain myself while in a low-paying job.

Ultimately the course of time comes to a head when all resources have been exhausted. We just simply run out of gas. —SM

As expected, the well became dry, and I found myself sluggishly back at my parents' home. My grandmother on my mother's side had moved into my old bedroom, so I had to share the basement with my two baby brothers, who were still residing with them. My parents had moved into another area of the city by this time, a Movin' On Up moment for them as the house was a fresh new build. It was a grandiose nine hundred square feet of living space with an unfinished basement, of which they did a quick fix of framing and drywalling as I required privacy being the only girl.

The house was seldom calm as my two younger brothers did not get along, and there was always a contention of strife between them. Alain, who was approximately sixteen years old at the time, was in an unusual and atypical stage of his life. He was very temperamental and seemed to be struggling with many internal conflicting emotions.

He had just converted from Catholicism to become a dedicated wholehearted Jehovah Witness. Although he and Paul shared the same bedroom all their lives, an adjoining bond never did take place between them. Now withstanding a new religious topic between them, arguments, fist fights, and verbal conflicts ended up separating them for a lifetime. Alain wasn't really close to anyone in my family other than a cousin he clung to, who had also converted to the same religion. I was delighted they had each other to lean on as my heart was broken, having a brother I loved but not being able to resolve the isolation and detachment we had with each other.

He left with what seemed like a "run away from home maneuver." With very little notice he was in British Columbia, where he resided for several years. There was minimal contact.

In the conclusion of his life he met a lovely French woman who shared the same faith, and he ultimately married her. They resided in Quebec where they had a son. At the age of forty-nine, on what should have been an ordinary morning, his wife found him breathless on the floor, and with all her adrenalized strength and efforts there was no life to be brought back. Like my father who died suddenly of an aneurysm it appeared the same generational curse was passed down to my baby brother Alain. Paul ended up with an aneurysm as well, but a surgery took care of that in 2013.

Paul was definitely experimenting with life when we moved to the Windsor Park home, a friendly neighborhood community. He came out of his shell and did a lot of partying and hanging out with friends. With the loss of jubilant years that most children have fond memories of, Paul found himself filling his heart with things that helped him escape the unsettling thoughts of the past. He became the funny guy, the joker, the one who could always make you laugh.

Sometimes the strongest among us are the ones who smile through silent pain, cry behind closed doors, and fight battles nobody knows about. —**unknown author**

9

Undone

It was a cold winter afternoon and I was excitably rehearsing a swanky jigging dance in my parents' basement. It was for the City of Winnipeg's annual "Festival du Voyageur" jigging competition. I was wearing handmade mukluks as the prop for this "one woman show" rehearsal. Both my mother and I were very exceptional dancers when it came to jigging. She was raised with her father playing violin, and her brother (my Uncle Marcel Meilleur) was quite well-known during these events with his fiddle playing. Way back in the day of black and white television screens, he was notorious as a self-made artist on the Don Messer show.

With the music loud, I was intense and on an invigorating moment of what I called bootlicking dancing. I was feeling solid and unshakable in my intoxicating "winning attitude." Out of nowhere, in the twinkle of an eye, a contrasting euphoria took place. The winning mindset I was focused on had now taken a sharp detour into an ambiguous reaction of terror.

Like an unforeseen step into quicksand, my confident moment turned into an unexpected stride that brought me straight to the ground. I heard a snap of some sort and while laying there on the cold basement floor; my mind was trying to recap the moments of what had just taken place. I had no pain, so why was I on the ground? As I looked carefully I realized my knee was dislocated and my leg appeared deformed.

My grandmother was upstairs and I screamed as loud as my voice and lungs would allow me. The shock by this time had worn off and it was no longer protecting me. By the time the ambulance arrived I was unable to endure the pain. I asked the paramedics to give me a form of relief, but none was given. It took approximately ten to fifteen minutes to reach the hospital. (An eternity, it seemed.) I remember the pain was so excruciating I didn't care if I lived or died. Nothing mattered anymore, and no one I loved was enough to keep me there alive. I just wanted to be knocked out.

I ended up in the hallway for hours on a stretcher waiting to be seen. Luckily on arrival I was given a painkiller (morphine) that took me from chaos to calm.

Finally I was taken into a room after several x-rays. A young doctor entered and spoke to me very eloquently about giving him an acknowledgement of consent for other interns to come in and watch. I agreed. The doctor and I were still alone at this time, and since the painkiller was wearing off, I was very anxious to move forward to the next procedure. (Whatever that was.)

I had been moved to a room that had many other beds, and the only privacy was cubicle curtains.

What happened next was very devastating and confusing. The doctor pulled the curtains shut and we were alone in this small space. I thought nothing unusual of it until he reached over and began to unbutton my blouse. I was eighteen years old and feeling very vulnerable. The doctor was someone I looked up to and trusted. He was the elite, the professional and the only one who could protect me and fix the problem. I asked, "What are you doing?"

I remained cool as I was afraid, intimidated and felt overpowered by him. He responded by telling me it was a prerequisite to include a regular checkup. "It really is not necessary," I told him. "My family physician took care of that several months ago. Other than this knee dislocation, I am in good health."

By this time he had almost every button on my blouse undone. Faint-hearted and stunned by this incident, I manage to muster enough strength to ask him to please stop. Although he was squeamishly reluctant, he pulled away.

Outside the thin murky curtains of this confined space, I heard voices of hospital staff going about their business with normalcy. On this side, I was being mishandled, humiliated and fearfully violated. The sound of someone speaking loudly was approaching, and a young intern opened one side of the curtains to say "Hello!" That was safety coming into my door. With a sigh of relief, there were several who came in the room and began to discuss with the doctor at my side if it was fine for them to stay.

He began to explain to them the diagnosis of my condition, and procedures I do not remember. His eyes eventually peered through mine, and he began to explain that if I counted to ten backwards I would shortly be asleep. I didn't trust him, and his face hardened when he turned towards me and away from them. He looked at me as though I was an insubordinate and defying individual. "Begin your count," he said. Ten, nine, eight … and then he grabbed my injured leg and began to adjust it while I was still awake. I leaped and screamed from the excruciating pain and then suddenly fell back onto the pillow. Out like a light!

I never saw this doctor again, nor did I ever tell anyone this experience. I felt ashamed, as though I had done something wrong. He had taken advantage of my vulnerability and was cognizant that I was young and naive. It was not something I brought on myself, but his actions towards me were as though I had.

I did not comply with him in my confused state, and this added exploitation was collectively adding up like a plaque in my heart. A violation, a thoughtless indiscretion of a moment, changed my trajectory to a mindset of unworthiness which lasted for many years.

I have learned that while those who speak about one's miseries usually hurt, those who keep silence hurt more. —**C.S. Lewis**

10

Suddenly

The summer before my knee dislocation was a warm and hot sunny season that most people seemed to be enjoying .While the rest of the world engaged in peace and quietness, and appreciating their vacations, I was busy playing tango with my low self-esteem, justifying if breaking up with John was a good idea. It didn't work out with Mathew and now I was struggling with John.

Coming home from working at my office (Merrill Lynch Royal Securities), I was driving over the Provencher Bridge in St. Boniface, and was just about to cross over a very busy intersection. There was a street light up ahead, but my mind had heedlessly shifted into an auto pilot mode long before I had left the office and got behind the wheel. It was 4:30 in the afternoon, and the sun was beaming with golden and luminous light in every direction. Although it was charmingly dispersing its warmth, I neither acknowledged nor received the invitation to admire its unblemished breath of light.

Suddenly …. The inside of my car was quickened to an unforeseen "darkness."

Was there a solar eclipse? It's not evening, is it? Hoonk Hoonk!!! What is that sound?

In haste I turned my head and followed the powerful and deafening horns.

It was as quick as the twinkle of an eye as the atmosphere of nightfall passionately gripped into my car.

The semi truck was dispatching its warning to me, and I was oblivious that the traffic light was now red. With my head space somewhere else, I drove right into the flowing traffic coming from the other direction.

How often do we get behind the wheel while our mind focuses on the cares of the world, then we ask ourselves arriving at our destination, "How did I get here?" (Auto-pilot!) —SM

I was right in the middle of the intersection, with no time to act. It was too late. The grill from a very large semi was now flush with my passenger window, blocking every vestige of light, and culminating in what seemed like a blackout. I will never forget the peculiarity of that grill; it was large, bold and worn-looking. And for a flash of time I was tormented in the premonition of knowing I was but a hairline away from a crash that would probably take my life.

Time froze right there, and I could never figure that out. There was for some reason time to question myself, and time to be angry with myself. A racing conversation took place in my mind, as I interrogated my stupidity and feeble-mindedness. Why was I not paying attention to the traffic? Why did I let John consume my mind? Was he worth the cost of my life? It was a slow-motion film as I reflected back to my hands on the wheel, turning my head to the right and seeing that grill, then lifting my head slightly to look upwards to the street light and seeing that it was red. By that time I should have been crushed and dragged across the intersection. But I wasn't! I was down the street safe and sound and perfectly parked.

Stunned beyond belief, I asked myself, "What just happened?" The traffic was smooth and flowing by me, while I was strangely and reluctantly calm. There was no human interpretation for this occurrence, or a science to refute the inevitable. Something or someone put me here. I looked back at the intersection and everything seemed normal, except I had a vision. My car was up in the air, and I saw a flowing white robe, whiter than snow and brighter than the sun, holding it up and taking it to where I was "*now*" quietly parked.

I was watching it like a movie on a screen in front of me.

In the New Testament, Mark chapter 4 - Jesus got up from the boat during a storm while the disciples were panicking and he rebuked the winds and said to the waves, "Quiet! Be still!" Then the wind died down and it was completely calm.

I felt this was a similar experience. Someone on my behalf spoke to death that day and proclaimed "Not today!"

For some strange reason I gripped the steering wheel in front of me with my head inclining towards it, repeating these words "Thank You Jesus, Thank you Jesus, and Thank you Jesus!"

I was not spiritual, only Catholic, if there was to be a difference! That day I saw the separation between the two and realized I had a glimpse of God, but did not see his face. No one ever taught me to say thank you to him other than to pray "Our father, who art in heaven." I knew that what had surprisingly come out of my mouth had to have been stirred up deep within my belly of emotions. Other than using the name of Jesus as a swear word, it just was not cool to say it this way. (At least not in my world or around any of my friends.)

11

Hitched

I married John. Walking down the aisle there was rivalry in my thoughts with every step. I had become a part-time model, working in the city with fashion shows, TV commercials, and some work on film as an extra. I drove myself to always look pretty and worked diligently at it, to prove I was not what my mother had implied I was.

Although today my mother fully regrets the power of her many words and implications towards me (such as "Only pretty girls dye their hair!"), they inevitably weighed deeply on me for a fragment of my journey. My focus was on becoming pretty, and the attention I was getting seemed to be the resolution, I profoundly thought.

Beauty is not who you are on the outside; it is the wisdom and time you gave away to save another struggling soul like you. —**Shannon L. Alder**

Approximately six months before the wedding, I woke up in the middle of the night in a wet bed. Wondering what was going on, I switched the light on, only to find out I was sitting in a pool of blood. My mother in the next room heard my scream and grabbed many towels, as I was increasingly hemorrhaging and was also submerged in blood. There was no time for an ambulance, so off I went with my dad holding towels and sheets between my legs to slow the flow.

By morning I was feeling very weak. They had controlled the blood flow by positioning me upwards from the waist down to allow the blood to clot. Everything from that point became cloudy; I could not recall a blood transfusion or the medical care given to me during the hours of my stay. My family physician, well-known for his demeaning attitudes towards women, entered the room. The fragrance of his arrogance was not unnoticed by anyone in his presence.

I have no memory of pushing, or if any medical implement was used to assist in the delivery of the undeveloped infant I was carrying. But I do avidly recall the photograph that hung on the walls of my mind, as the strange shaped blood clot with stringy shoots was transparently sealed in a glass jar.

"Well, you're not pregnant anymore!" Then the doctor theatrically raised the jar above his shoulders for all to see.

That portrait and those scripted words out of his mouth crumbled whatever disposition of strength and courage was left in my holding tank. I had never seen anyone other than my grandfather deceased, and that was an eerie view of his open coffin. I was now looking at a deformed baby with no name and no identity. To the doctor it was considered a devalued ball of mass that was ultimately going to be thrown away.

It's agony if you have to carry a baby in your heart rather than in your arms. —**Saying goodbye.org**

John and I moved forward from there, married and then separated four years later. His family background was a convolution of unusual family ties. One day on an easy-going Saturday afternoon while we were stilled married, John decided to drop in on his parents to visit. I stayed home to putter around as I needed to finish some spring cleaning. The house phone rang, and it was John. He had been there but an hour, and had a new sounding demeanor in his tone. He was excited and astounded about the mind-blowing and cutting edge news he just discovered about his family. He managed to sputter the words out but I couldn't believe it myself.

He explained there was a knock on the door at his parents. He opened the door and asked the tall 30ish year old man, "Can I help you?" "Yes you can," said the man. "I'm your half brother! My father lives here and has not seen me or my other four siblings since I was a child." John invited him in, and his mother looked pale and ready to faint. When John's mother met his father he had been married with five children. They had an affair, the father left his then wife and the five children to be with John's mother. They eventually married and had five children of their own, which included John, the second oldest. This was a very difficult day for John's mom, who thought these five other children, the ex-wife, and the secret past was dormant, never to awaken.

There are no secrets that time does not reveal.
—Jean Racine

11

Up-to-Here

Enough is enough! Being married to John was four years that felt like twenty. Drugs and alcohol became an ongoing controversial concern in our lives. Especially drugs, as alcohol was something I eventually joined in on to score a few winning points in pleasing him.

He was a daily pot smoker when I met him; nevertheless, on our last day together we had a vociferous exchange of words about his use of hash and cocaine in our home. We now had a beautiful daughter and I no longer wanted her exposed to this life. It was a losing battle for me as I knew he would never give up his drugs.

I perhaps reacted too soon to a situation in the heat of the moment, as it was not the first time he hit me or physically pushed me around for something I said.

I remember being frustrated, and walking over to our bedroom dresser, where he held his stash in a confined small area of the top drawer. I grabbed it, and made my way to the washroom and flushed it down the toilet where I made my statement. Enough!

– sick and tired of –

With my boldness in one hand and an empty bag of pot in the other, this was, in his mind, a confrontation for a brawl. When I heard his foot hit the ground from our bed I knew I was in a lot of trouble. I grabbed my one-year-old daughter, who was playing on the floor, and I desperately ran to hide in another room. Unfortunately, I didn't make the timing in getting the door closed fast enough as he kicked it open abruptly, and my daughter's head was hit from that force.

The impact of what he did brought him to a screeching halt. My daughter was screaming and crying simultaneously, as her instinct revealed that this environment held no safety for her.

It wasn't the first time John had remorse about his recurring temper. On one occasion I had minced too many words for his liking and it caused him to grab me by the throat and thrust me against the wall. That was a fearful moment for me as I knew there was no rationalizing. His fiery stoned red eyes indicated he had smoked pot and mixed it with other drugs. I had to seal my mouth and let him holler till he was ready to let me go. Any provocation from me at that time could have easily changed the course of this situation to a severe criminal matter.

The memories begin to flood back in, while he had me pinned up against the kitchen wall. My lips were sealed and my mouth was fixed shut. He was angry and accusing me of speaking even though I wasn't. Just like the day I had a nightmare and lay on the cold laminate floor, wedging my little fingers under my parent's bedroom door. I was hoping to get closer to them but fearful to make a sound in case I woke and angered them. Just like the time my lips were sealed and fixed shut when my ex-fiancé Mathew pinned me down to a chair and hovered over me.

Now here I was again, broken, afraid, and shutting down.

Those memories helped me to stay quiet and submissive while I was waiting out the wave of his anger to wind down. Finally his eyes changed and became warm and teary. The remorse was too much for his heart, and he broke down like a sobbing child who cannot catch his breath. His nose was running, and I quickly came to his aid, to comfort him in his sorrow.

Although there were many "I'm sorrys" from him, I found myself to be the backbone of our relationship, always comforting him, with no one securing or protecting me during his violent rages.

Author Laura Davies articulates well how a young girl who is abused reacts, in her book "Allies in Healing." It's very relative to how an adult woman feels and reacts when a man abuses her.

Abuse manipulates and twists a child's natural sense of trust and love. Her innocent feelings are belittled or mocked, and she learns to ignore her feelings. She can't afford to feel the full range of feelings in her body while she's being abused — pain, outrage, hate, vengeance, confusion, arousal. So she short-circuits them and goes numb. For many children, any expression of feelings, even a single tear, is cause for more severe abuse. Again, the only recourse is to shut down. Feelings go underground. —**Laura Davis**

I waited till my husband left for work and called my father. He came to my aid quickly, with my older brother, and they threw everything I owned in a truck. With that, I walked away from this marriage.

Unfortunately I was only able to stay at my parents for a few days. "You made your bed, now lie in it" were my mother's words. It sounds insensitive, but she was part of that "tough love" generation where they were still trying to figure out the boundaries of how much affection they should be distributing to their children and/or how much money, room and board etc, etc. I ended up making my way to a women's shelter but didn't last the day. A colleague from where I used to work heard of my situation and stepped up to the plate, providing me shelter.

I was so happy to have a roof over my head that I never once complained about watching her sniff cocaine every night. Even in front of my one year old daughter.

Here I was running away from my offender yet exposing my daughter to the same environment, just without the abuser. I could have given up hope very easily, and I wanted to, but for some divine reason there always seemed to be something for me to hang on to that prevented me from spiraling downhill.

This woman was my night in shining armor. Her provision was, to me, a step up the stairway in avoiding homelessness.

I was living in an old rundown apartment with rodents, cockroaches, little food, and I was depressed and lonely. To add to this hardship my heart sank into my stomach when I found out I was pregnant with another child.

Life has a way of testing a person's will, either by having nothing happen at all or by having everything happen at once. —**Paulo Coelho**

With a few friends in my circle, "abortion" was the enchanting and soothsaying word. It was the answer to knocking off one of the burdens that had just piled up on my mountain of troubles. One day while researching abortion options, I glanced over to my daughter, admiring her beautiful smile, and realized that someone just like her was living in me. Falling on my knees, broken-hearted and with my hands embracing my stomach, I desperately clung to feel that life. Suddenly a warm peaceful feeling came over me and a new thinking pattern evolved. Even with all the reasoning as to why I should get an abortion, as it certainly was warranted according to my friends, I couldn't wrap my heard around it anymore. Their continued efforts to remind me I was not capable, both emotionally and physically, to deal with another child was an accurate observation. But something was going on in my heart that passed all understanding, and this uncommon peace I was strangely experiencing pushed me forward to say "no."

Once that unnerving season was dealt with, my parents stopped in to see me one day. They were taken aback by the conditions I was living in. My mother's trigger response was "OMG, we are taking you back home!" She helped pack what little my daughter and I had, and we lived with my parents till I was able to collect a government social assistance allowance. (No one would hire me while I was pregnant and I was too much of an emotional mess.)

13

Stranger

In hindsight I could see decisions, small or great, change the course of my life.

Ironically, the smallest decisions we make in our lives can sometimes be the ones that change our life path forever, and those larger decisions we lose sleep over can often become the least in effecting any change at all. —SM

I strongly believe that Jesus said it best when he simply said "Be anxious for nothing!" This was something I did not stitch to my heart, and it cost me greatly.

With all the tears that marriage put me through, it was a reminder to me that I was perhaps a failure in many things. Even though I was an overcomer, I didn't believe it, based on all the circumstances around me that made me feel like I was sinking, not climbing. Leaving him was the right thing to do, in order to be free from the abuse. I wanted to be positive, not to worry and move forward, but I just didn't know how to master my thoughts. And so I continued the off and on thinking that mostly leaned on replaying the past in my head.

If we could picture one's heart through some form of x-ray to see pain, I know there would be a black scar in the corner of mine. When I reflect back to my marriage with John, I am cognizant of a puzzling and hurtful disheartening memory.

When we were married less than a year, I remember John had called me from work one day and said he wasn't coming home. He wouldn't tell me where, how, why, nothing!

I didn't see him for three days.

We lived in a small apartment at the time, and there wasn't a lot of room for pacing the floor, but I did it anyway. Where was my husband? What is he doing? Why did he leave me? What did I do wrong? How can I fix this? It was the longest three days of my life. I slept alone, looking at all his belongs as though he was still here cuddled next to me. How did we go from a normal day at the office to this? My mind was restless and I couldn't eat or sleep. On day three the door opened and he walked in with ease. "Hi babe, I'm so sorry," he says. "I'll never do that again, and please don't ask any questions." Don't ask any questions? "Where were you?" I demanded.

Seeing his demeanor change to a vexatious temperament I knew I had to back off. I made my way into the kitchen, made supper and pretended as if nothing unusual had happened. Something I had been trained to do in this marriage many times.

With all the turmoil of emotions I was entangled in, John's mother always dispersed warmth and tenderness towards me. She was beautiful and graceful. Unfortunately pancreatic cancer swallowed her up at the early age of fifty-six.

Prior to her death, we visited her frequently in the hospital. At that time, children were not allowed to be around patients, and so like detectives we tucked our baby girl under John's jacket, and pulled the zipper. It was a perfect fit.

John's mom had her last day with our daughter holding her while teary eyed. She was counting the days of her life, knowing they were ending soon, and the thought of never seeing her granddaughter grow up kept her coddling her for hours till her arms gave way. She was not only my mother-in-law, but a woman who was broken in her marriage as well, and I felt connected to her in so many ways. I loved her dearly and miss her so very much. The two children I had with John will never know their incredible grandmother, who would have purposed herself to live for them.

Leaving John while his mother was sick was never an option; however, the day came when I drew my line in the sand as I mentioned in the earlier chapter.

Soon my second child was born. He had a type of infant death syndrome disease and would often stop breathing. I had to sit him up and never lay him down as that would put him at risk. He had colic and cried night and day for weeks on end.

John spent very little time with our daughter and would not acknowledge throughout my pregnancy that I was carrying his second child. On December 1st 1982, the day our son was born, he surprised me with flowers in the hospital and asked to meet his son.

When our children were the ages of six and four he decided to walk away from them. He was never dedicated to seeing them, and this made it easier for him to remove the weight of any responsibility towards them. He wanted me to drop the court order of his $200.00 a month child support, and promised to remove himself from our lives. (Which he did.)

He remarried, and his new wife did end up calling me years later. She had left him, and wanted to validate a few things with me concerning him. She asked me if he had ever grabbed my hair and dragged me with it. He had done many things, I told her, but that wasn't one of them. It was clear to me what he had done to her. We had shared the same thread of brokenness that was brought on to us by the same man.

14

On The Skids

Living apart from the man you love is like walking a pathway of shrubbery and bristles. Although there are surface scratches, there is a sensation of freedom when you finally get through it. —SM

Walking away from an abusive relationship, whether physical or emotional, takes a toll on the mind and body. I was pulling through one day then falling apart the next. I struggled with getting a grip on balance. Perhaps I had tilted the scale without knowing how to bring it to a normal level. Whatever that was! I was contending with many trapped feelings, with no more room to store them. So I just stirred up what I had, not knowing any better.

I have since learned there is simply no immediate cure or remedy when breaking away from an abusive relationship. The healing process of time must be embraced to avoid the scars. This can be done by YOU loving YOU!

For me, part of that restoration was purposely observing the beauty around me. Pulling out the ugly weeds of my thoughts and finding the two flowers to focus on, my daughter and my son. As both my children developed over the years I detected many familiar characteristics of their estranged biological father. John was fascinated with photography and became professional at it. Although my daughter never saw her father after seven years old, she too ended up enchanted with photography. She possesses her father's charismatic smile with those perfect heart-shaped lips she inherited from him. My son has the equivalent warm-hearted laugh as John, and I still at times get startled when I hear it.

Although this is a fast-forward to the first two children I had, there was a dark hole in between where the cognition of suicide knocked on my door more than once. Backing up to my first attempt, I was seventeen years old when an uncle of mine walked into my bedroom unexpectedly. This was very unusual for him, as he rarely visited us. For some strange reason he wanted to pop in to say hi. We startled each other as he was not expecting to find me with a handful of aspirins ready to swallow. He was never my favorite uncle, but he saved my life with nothing more than an hour's pep talk. Although my parents did not intentionally withdraw affection from me, they simply did not know how to give it. Even between them there was very little public display of it. Who could live without a hug, a kiss or encouragement? I felt absent to my parents and it made me invisible to myself.

The second time I contemplated ending my life, I lived alone with my two small children. At that time John had not remarried yet, and rumors were he had a new girl on his arm at the bar almost every night. Nothing unusual as I remember John had dreamed of being a musician and was always practicing on his drums.

– Pipe dream –

He wanted to hang out with musicians and spent most of his weekends at the bar. His goal was to play in a band with his best friend, who was a seasoned bass player. When John and I were together his friend continually dropped in to drink. Because his friend always had a kind manner towards me, I reciprocated same, and never showed my anger.

John's friend moved forward to play with a popular Canadian band that still have their hits on the radio today. Unfortunately, alcohol became the transgressor that controlled his life, and he died in March of 2015. At his funeral I was privileged to sit behind his family, and we had the opportunity to reminisce about years past. John did not attend.

During the time John was out enjoying his new single life, I was at home spiraling downwards with my two small children. My quality of life was reduced to collecting welfare, smoking two packs of cigarettes a day, and popping valium. To add to this grief-stricken idleness, I now lived in a low-income housing complex. Could life get any better? Probably not!

My children were quietly playing in their room and I selfishly grabbed a razor blade, thinking I could end my life, right here, right now. I began to scratch the surface of my wrist, which was to be the practice run in a grand finale of slashing through my vein.

Like a knock on the door, there was that subtle voice again rising up deep within my belly to the pounding of my heart. It was "Love" for myself, mounting up to tell me I was worthy to live. I disposed of all the razor blades, grabbed a few bandages for my wrist, held my children, and then threw myself on my bed. I cried for hours.

With these emotions escalating, I eventually ended up with agoraphobia, panic disorder and anxiety attacks. For almost one year I was housebound.

The Merriam Webster dictionary describes agoraphobia this way: "An abnormal fear of being helpless in a situation from which escape may be difficult or embarrassing that is characterized initially often by panic or anticipatory anxiety and finally by avoidance of open or public places."

Panic disorder and panic attacks are defined by the Mayo Clinic as a sudden episode of intense fear that triggers severe physical reactions when there is no real danger or apparent cause. Panic attacks can be very frightening. When panic attacks occur, you might think you're losing control, having a heart attack or even dying.

Like a vehicle stuck in the mud spinning its wheels, was my life's narrative and classic description.

15

The Race

Lying on my frayed and time-worn sofa one day, I was watching my two children playing on the floor close beside me. I began to daydream, and wandered into my thoughts where my cloud of "happier days" were, in the hopes of finding "me" once again.

I used to drive a warm tan color standard transmission, Formula 400 Pontiac Firebird. I had a friend at the time who loved cruising with me on weekends through Winnipeg city streets. We had so much attention in this fast car. My blonde hair and her sophisticated European look unquestionably made the boys chase us down while we were driving.

At red lights they would rev their engines. My crazy girlfriend would urge me to do the same, and so I would happily oblige. At the green light the race was on. It was like I had nothing to lose. I would race them in their sporty lavish cars, and I usually won! I was very fast and drove at crazy speeds while shifting without using the clutch. I managed to impress many guys with this skill, and my girlfriend and I ultimately shared many laughs on our cruising adventures. I suppose it helped my self-esteem which I was lacking so much of at the time.

I remember watching in my rear view mirror one time, while a candy apple red Camero crashed dead onto a parked car. I was so used to having these suave guys pull up to me at red lights revving their engines to play the chicken game, it started to feel like it was part of having a normal day at the office. I didn't have much money at seventeen but I sure drove a winning car that year. One warm Sunday afternoon my girlfriend and I were chatting in my car while driving, and we stopped at a red light. Nothing unusual until this really cool Camero pulled up beside us, and the driver with his passenger friend started whistling and blowing kisses our way. With his flirty wink and rev of the engine it was an indisputable invitation to drag race. Still waiting at the red light, I leaned over to discuss the next move with my friend. "

These guys just want to prove some form of their testosterone power," she said, "so do it!" Clearly he would have to have a good head start, as the lane that I was in was clear of any vehicles. But the lane he was in had a parked car half a block up. All bets were on! He thought he was going to beat me at the line, and eventually cut in front of me and miss that parked car. But It was a miscalculation on his part as my car beat him at the line and left him in the dust. I was too proud to slow down and let him in my lane now that we both knew I was clearly the winner, and he was too proud to slow down with his determination to win.

Inevitably he crashed straight into that parked car. I will never forget how spellbound I was watching in my rear view mirror the hood of that brand new car crunching up. Fortunately no one was hurt, and being so young and foolish, my friend Michelle and I had great laughs over this for many years.

Lying on the sofa with the kids still playing close by me, the happier times I was theorizing about just "burst" when my son tapped me on the shoulder to ask for something to drink. "Those days are gone," was the voice in my head as I made my way to the refrigerator. By the time I poured my son's juice, another panic attack came over me and I rushed to find my valium to calm me down.

I had been offered shock treatments by one practitioner, and several options for anti-depressants by another. I didn't like how the anti-depressants made me feel, and I most certainly declined the shock treatments without hesitation. Perhaps it was my own stubbornness or my egotism that caused me to believe there had to be more alternatives. Although shock treatments have proven to be successful with some patients, it wasn't my preferred selection to the long-lasting cure. I worked diligently at overcoming this mental illness by practicing daily leaving the house with valium in my pocket.

It was a triumphant victory if I made it to the grocery store. Unfortunately once I was in the store, I would stop and consider, should I ask someone to call an ambulance? Scream for help? My preferred choice was to go back home as fast as I could. Little lies in my head deceived me into believing that my house was the only place for refuge and safety, or that I was having a heart attack.

A violent aggression of emotion would have its way over me with the trepidation of terror. I just couldn't breathe when that happened. Sadly, even when I conquered walking into any building outside of home, I was often hit with another anxiety attack as a result of crowds of people, and the claustrophobic effect that would always trigger in me. I would somehow compose myself with a lot of self-talk, sweat hard, grab what I needed for groceries, and pop another valium. It was burdensome as I shared with very few people my predicament. I played the role of being ok. I knew in the background some family and friends implicated me as a victim collecting social assistance to avoid working. Nothing was further from the truth. I was never a lazy individual, just someone suffering from emotional disorders based on what happened to me.

Over time I made a choice to get better. I decided I would fight to get my life back. This came about when my two-year-old son managed to open the front storm door and ran out. With a prevailing motherly instinct there was no hesitation in running after him. I caught up with him two neighbors down, and grabbed him. A sensation of relief came over me, but for only a moment. I had forgotten I was outside, but when the realization kicked in without a warning, a manifesting panic attack set me off. Once again I was fighting for my breath, and did not simmer down till I was shielded from the outdoors and safe in my house. Being outside was the colossal giant I had to face every day.

– I think I can make it –

I reached out for help and found a program called COPE, which I believe was through an anxiety disorder association. Leaving my house was hard but I pushed myself through it, even though I thought I might stop breathing. I was very ashamed of my life, and came up with all kinds of reasons why I would not leave my home. Putting on the television set one day, a physician was explaining to a live audience that when a panic attack strikes and you feel like you can't breathe, you should jump up and down. "If you physically can't breathe," he said, " you won't be able to do this." That was a trajectory mindset change for me. I knew at some point during the day I would have an anxiety attack, and was looking forward to trying this out. Sure enough, I was jumping up and down in the midst of my anxiety and still, I was breathing. Since it took my mind off the anxiety in part, I found myself with a new attitude of "I am going to win this battle."

The beginning of a race!

Fact One: Races are won or lost in key moments. Fact Two: Success in the sport is, above all else, about enduring suffering. **—Chris McCormack**

16

Unexpected

I wasn't ready to race anything, but the starting line was where I was headed. Like a born again experience everything was going to be fresh and new. A switch came on and it came down to choices.

A cousin of mine was a Christian and she would call me from time to time to talk. She wanted to pray with me on the phone and so she led me in a prayer that helped me to understand that there was a God that loved me and all I had to do was receive that love in my life. It was a warm and kind prayer that resulted in bending my knees and shedding a few tears. Once I hung up the phone I continued life as usual.

I had to find strength somewhere to get better. My two children gave me the vitality to push forward because they were the main purpose of my life and I loved them so much (even though I was a mess). I worked hard so that they would not recognize that something was emotionally wrong with their mother. I didn't want them feeling neglected, but I am sure they did. Weaning myself off of valium was a slow journey. It was a long haul to finally leave my house and not need to take a pill each time.

I began reading books – something I had never done. I read so many self-help books I was running out of storage space for them. The book "Love" by Leo Buscaglia was a turning point which helped me to understand human relationships better. It was the first book I purchased to read when I decided to change the direction of my life.

Leo Buscaglia led a free, non-credit class at the University of Southern California in the 60's and 70's and he called it the "Love Class."

He opened his first class with this introduction:

In the winter of 1969, an intelligent, sensitive female student of mine committed suicide. She was from a seemingly fine upper middle class family. Her grades were excellent. She was popular and sought after. On the particular day in January she drove her car along the cliffs of Pacific Palisades in Los Angeles, left the motor running, walked to the edge of a deep cliff overlooking the sea and leaped to her death on the rocks below. She left no note, not a word of explanation. She was only twenty.

I have never been able to forget her eyes; alert, alive, responsive, full of promise. I can even recall her papers and examinations which I always read with interest. I wrote on one of her papers which she never received, "A very fine paper. Perceptive, intelligent and sensitive. It indicates your ability to apply what you have learned to your 'real' life. Nice work!" What did I know about her "real" life?

I often wondered what I would read in her eyes or her papers if I could see them now. But, as with so many people and situations in our life, we superficially experience them, they pass and can never be experienced in the same manner.

... I simply wondered what I might have done; if I could have, even momentarily, helped.

On page 95 he writes, "To love others you must first love yourself."

Leo Buscaglia states love has been ignored by the scientists, and that you can only give away what you have. He claims the word "love" is rarely found in psychology books or any other academic books.

The book "Love" by Leo Buscaglia and "Pilgrim's Progress" by John Bunyan are the two most valuable books that helped to shape my thinking. From beginning to end, they leave you wanting change in your life. At least for me it was one of the most influential revelations in the capturing of a new mindset.

With this new way of thinking I was beginning to break free. Routine was back in my life with a new job, and kids were comfortably enjoying daycare. I was free from medication but still not out of the struggle. I was broke but happier. I was able to take in deep breaths outside without panic, go for walks, and be back in the work field like the rest of the world. Although this was affirming, I was still at war internally with depression and anxiety. They knocked on my door to get back in like a ball and chain. It was that on-purpose thinking I talked about in the earlier chapters that pushed me forward in staying true to my mindset.

For God did not give me a spirit of fear, but of power, and of love, and of a "SOUND" mind. This was something I had read in a "Daily Bread" Christian pamphlet one day, and I cut it out and carried it with me, and read it every time I felt like I was going back to that deep hole I was living in.

Although I had a full-time job, I was asked to work as a part-time model, and so I guardedly joined an agency. My pre-eminent concern was the upfront cost. I happened to know the photographer working for them, and fortunately was able to get a portfolio for very little money.

I landed a few gigs in television commercials, some work as an extra in a few movies, and lots of runway work for large department stores. I was not able to put more time or effort into it as my paychecks were well secured in my full-time job, and I had two children to feed. A bookkeeper in a popular franchised store was not something anyone expected I could do as I was terrible in math, but I pulled it off.

⟫◦⟪

17

Old One-Two

While at work the owner's son would drop into my office frequently to check on something in our office filing drawers. His cologne scent and his warm smile were just enough to get my attention. He was soft-spoken, sophisticated, and smooth with the ladies. The girls in the office would repeatedly babble on about him being a good catch. He never seemed to get to work on time, but everyone would watch as he pulled up in his brand new golden Porsche, his suave attire ready to impress us all!

He seemed very intrigued with me, and we spent a lot of time talking in the lunch room during our coffee breaks. It wasn't long before we embarked on exploring a few date nights. I would suggest meeting him somewhere, as I was still living in a complex for fixed income and I was sure he would lose interest in me if he knew. And this is exactly what happened. He was over at my home only twice to meet my children and to spend those evenings with us. He was very uncomfortable both times, for two reasons. He didn't want to date someone who had children, and although he didn't express it verbally, I knew in my heart it also had to do with my living situation of poverty and hardship.

He eventually told me he could not introduce me to his mother as she told him to be with someone who was more ambitious, and without children. I remember how hurtful it felt to hear those words. His family were considered to be the "financially secured," and the "well to do" as the cliché goes! (Material things, cocktail parties and the who's who.)

Do not judge me by my successes, judge me by how many times I fell down and got back up again.
—Nelson Mandela

I eventually met someone else through a friend. He was Jewish and he too wouldn't introduce me to his mother. But this time it was because my background was Christian and not of the Jewish faith. To his credit, however, he was somewhat supportive when I shared with him what I had come out of.

He seemed to enjoy my two children when he was visiting, but that would only last but an hour. "I'm not really sure if I want children yet but I really enjoy your company," he would say. He had an alluring sense of humor, which I appreciated in our relationship as it compensated for my periodic intense posture. He knew how to make me laugh.

However, the prevailing day did arrive, as I knew it would. He pulled up in a brand new 2-seater sports car. Like it was yesterday I remember my question to him standing in the parking lot. How do you expect me to go for a ride with you? The kids are too small to be alone and your car will never accommodate them. I should have been happy for him, because he was so excited. For me, I saw the bigger picture and it didn't include my children, so I ended the relationship that day.

I moved on to a better paying job as a receptionist for a water company. The owner would often bring in his friends, and there I met my second husband to be. He was a bit of a joker around me, and I was very attracted to anyone who could make me laugh. He enjoyed socializing one on one and in large groups. In the evenings after work he was busy hanging out with friends and living a single life. I was busy working, going home, tending to the kids and off to bed to start all over the next day following the same routine. Being in bed by seven in the evening was not unusual for me as the stress of depression, agoraphobia and panic attacks had long stressed me and I needed at least twelve hours of sleep to play catch up in my life. Smoking two packs of cigarettes a day was very stimulating, yet I found it somewhat relaxing. This was a contradiction in itself. I ended up with various compulsive and addictive behaviors, which is not uncommon working through any mental illness, or even depression. The cigarette became my friend in the broken times and ingenuous times.

Let me lose everything on earth and the world beyond, but let me not lose what I'm craving for, let it be that I died on the way than retreating from getting it.
—Michael Bassey Johnson

I have learned that one of two things happen to people who have been neglected or hurt. Either they end up with a sense of entitlement where they think the world owes them, or they make their own path and include helping others as they deal with what they've gone through. I chose the latter.

– Back at the water company –

The boss's friend routinely dropped in, and it was mostly to see me. We eventually started to date but it was more like him hanging out at my house. For me there was no real attraction at the beginning. He was always in front of me and I couldn't seem to make him go away. Even when I didn't take his calls he would show up at my door with bags of groceries and treats for the kids. I was very predictable in terms of my whereabouts, as home and work were the only two places I would likely be. My life was simple, but it had to be in order for me to heal properly.

I never wanted to forget how fortunate I was to have regained the ability to do what most people take for granted, like walking outside. Something I previously couldn't do without drugs in my body. Now that I was getting out of the gate of that prison, it was so easily out of my mind once I conquered it.

A mother forgets her labor pains once her child is born, so much so that she does it again. Each time telling herself, this is the last time! **—SM**

18

Round The Bend

I saw an ad one day in the newspaper and it gave me an idea for a career. I explored it further and ended up quitting my job and went to a school of cosmetology to get my license in Aesthetics. I qualified to receive a student loan that included government allowances for daycare, books, and living expenses. My new boyfriend was a real help in this as he always insisted on picking up the kids at the daycare for me at the end of the day. This was my first clue that I needed to start doing some things on my own again as he was always there, and it got to the point where I really needed him all the time. I was becoming co-dependent while trying to be independent. I had so many needs it was hard to say no when he offered to help.

A new shift was around the corner and I was finally moving out of the fixed income housing complex. Based on the color of the block, my kids used the term "the green houses!" Nevertheless, I was movin' on up! What a prodigious production to my senses, to feel like I'd made it and could now abandon my past to move forward. Of course, the new boyfriend helped me to move, and to purchase groceries, and he did anything else I wanted him to. I couldn't manage without him in my life as he had set himself up pretty good in being part of my routine. I did not become a part of his life but rather he submerged into mine and he was now joined to it.

My life became full and busy from dusk till dawn. There was no one else in my life but him and so when he asked me to marry him it just seemed natural to say yes. I wasn't in love; I was just being practical, which I thought was an adult thing to do.

It was one day at a time and everything seemed ordinary, which was calming for me but not exciting. I wasn't feeling that "in love" sensuality with my fiancé, but I undeniably loved the idea of not being alone. He really was helpful with the kids and with my ongoing "things to do list." He covered it every time. Unfortunately we didn't talk very much with each other on intimate or deep level issues, and so I felt disheartened often. Even when we married it was like being with a stranger. He didn't get me, and perhaps I didn't get him.

A few months prior to my wedding day an unexpected phone call changed the mundane to bizarre. I had met this guy during the time I lived in the low income housing complex. A group of women I was associated with introduced me to him. I can't recall how they knew him other than he would show up downtown regularly where I was setting up a woman's gym called "Fitness Now." I had no idea what I was doing but I dove into this business plan and went as far as charging for memberships and hiring an instructor, whom I started paying monthly.

Things were moving so fast I had not even registered the business name. I clearly was reversed in my business smarts. I simply didn't have any. One day walking through a department store a woman began to holler and swear at me in front of all the patrons. She couldn't reach me by phone to get her cash back, as I never opened the business after all, yet I had collected fees on some early bird memberships.

This woman was raging furious with me. I told her that I had to walk away, and apologetically expressed my failure in the business. It was uncomfortable and embarrassing for me. I remained humbled to her and took her phone number down.

I made a promise to return her money, which I did in small payments.

I wasn't heartless, I just didn't know what to do when It was costing me so much and I felt there was no other option than to close the doors on a business that never really got started. In the end she understood what I was going through, and accepted my apology. *Whew!*

***It takes many good deeds to build a good reputation, and only one bad one to lose it.* —Benjamin Franklin**

Getting back to the call from a guy that kept dropping in at my gym that never opened, it's an interesting memoir to tell. I just remember him hanging around a lot and when I was no longer there I assumed he had his own life and I would probably never see him again.

Breaking

– The phone rang –

It was him! His name was Dennis. He wanted to say hi and asked if he could drop in at my apartment for a visit. He seemed nice enough, and harmless. Although he was somewhat a stranger to me, I didn't feel threatened by him and so I agreed. My fiancé on the other hand was uncomfortable with me being alone with him especially while my two children would be in bed by the time Dennis would arrive. My fiancé was out of town at the time.

I put the kids to bed and there was a knock on the door. I recognized him through the peephole and graciously let him in. Holding a charming white and decorative bedside lamp in his hands he pronounced "Here is a present for you!" A little unusual for a gift, I thought, but I cheerfully accepted it.

The evening was odd and I found him somewhat peculiar, but who was I to judge him on the weirdness? However, that feeling did trigger me to ask him a few questions, and I became investigative like an ombudsman would. Speaking freely with no inhibitions in his soft spoken voice he stated "I'm schizophrenic." Staying calm without reacting, I asked him if he was on medication. He avoided the question by giving me the report of his diagnosis, and wanted to educate me so I could be comfortable with it and understand him better. I truly believe he meant well and seemed to be looking for a friend, but I felt it was escalating into a delusional feeling he might be having about me. I ended our visit rather quickly, explaining to him that I had to get up early the next morning.

He called me several times after that, but due to the uneasiness I felt around him, I avoided him as much as I could. I would often bring up my fiancée's name on the phone to remind him I'm not available. Since I wasn't sure of his motives, I was always polite to him. One evening I heard outside my 2nd storey building the sound of a car's horn, then another, then another. It was him; he was yelling at the top of his lungs for my attention in hopes I could hear him.

No guitar in his hands serenading me, this was an aggressive maneuver to get my attention. He was in a brand new black slick car which I knew he did not own, as he only commuted through public transportation, and he was unemployed at the time. Clearly he could not afford this vehicle. I became frightened and did not feel safe. I immediately grabbed both of my children, put their coats and shoes on then retreated from my suite and into the hallway. I could hear the main door at the bottom of the stairs open and heavy footsteps coming up to the upper level. Holding the hands of my children on both sides of me, I quickly began to go down the stairs at the opposite end of the building. But it was too late as he was already behind me.

I put on a great performance. "Hi Dennis, how are you? Sorry, we were just leaving to meet up with friends." "I saw you look out the window," he said. "Oh! That was you?" As I sounded so surprised, "I heard a ruckus down there with loud music and it looked like someone was hollering, but it was so dark outside I was not able to see clearly."

"I want you to come and see my new car," he said. "Oh sure," I replied, "but just for a moment. We really must be going."

My two children who were oblivious to what was going on seemed both excited, and perplexed at the same time.

We made our way to this fantastic show case vehicle. "Get in," he said. I stalled him with questions and asked "Where did you get this car?" "I'm on a test drive," he said, "from a dealership." "Which dealership?" I asked. He mentioned the name of a town that was a half hour's drive from the city. My stomach wasn't feeling very good, and I was trying to figure out how to run.

I quickly made up a story, and told him I was picking up my brother and making my way to a restaurant. He continued to manipulate the conversation about getting me and my children in the car, by offering himself as chauffeur.

I stood my ground, but it all got twisted and before I knew it, I was dropping my kids off at my parents for safety then I actually did pick up my brother. We made our way to the restaurant, and Dennis met us there.

I told the story to my brother as we commuted to the restaurant, and we devised a plan. "Paul," I said, "you will excuse yourself to go to the washroom and then call the police about this apologue. I called my fiancé, who also joined us at the restaurant. My brother made the call, then came back to the table. The police never came. Everyone was playing dumb, and we talked about nothing, just to pass the time. No one mentioned the car in the parking lot that Dennis presumably stole.

The restaurant was closing down and the waiter was laboring hard on the subtle hints. "We are now closed!" Why didn't the police show up? Hey, where is everyone going? My fiancé offered a ride to my brother because it was on the way for him. And so there I was, left alone with Dennis.

The night seemed content without trouble, and since the police didn't show up, everyone just assumed it was probably nothing. Everyone but me!

With the restaurant closing, there were only a few cars left in the parking lot. The overhead lights were dim and I felt uneasy once again. My fiancé had parked in the front or on another street close by and no one thought to stay with me. (They thought I was probably over reacting.) There I was, alone with Dennis again. "Well good night, talk to you soon!" I said.

I figured I would just get in my car and go home. I felt defeated, in that my instincts might be wrong about this guy, or I was the only one who saw through this awkward situation that something really was wrong. Taking a few steps towards my car, Dennis shouted, "Hey, get in my car. You owe me to take you for a ride." "Oh it's too late," I said. He became more aggressive in his volume and asserted once again, "GET in the car!"

I didn't have a chance to respond as I was stunned by a group of men who suddenly jumped over a fence that was close by. They headed straight for us. I was pushed out of the way by one of them, and Dennis was already pinned to the ground by two of the others. The trunk was flung open and I saw many different shaped boxes, including one containing a lamp that was similar to the one he had given me. Did these boxes have drugs or explosives? So much was going through my mind and I didn't know what to make of it. In an aggressive tone I heard someone say to me "Get in your car please, and leave." I think it was the police or some sort of SWAT team. In a nervous manner I complied, but I was still perplexed. With a racing heart I wondered, "What just happened?" I was young and naïve so I just carried on the next day trying to avoid the feelings of being traumatized as I believe I was. I have often thought to myself, "Did I get saved from something that could have harmed my life?" I never heard from him again.

19

Go-For

The experience with Dennis left me with a humble and most grateful attitude. In my research on schizophrenia I realized that I myself had escaped this convoluting mental illness. Since schizophrenia's known causes are not merely genetic I was not surprised to find they included environmental issues as well.

Wikipedia describes Schizophrenia this way:

Schizophrenia is a mental disorder characterized by abnormal social behavior and failure to understand what is real. Common symptoms include false beliefs, unclear or confused thinking, hearing voices, reduced social engagement and emotional expression, and a lack of motivation. People with schizophrenia often have additional mental health problems such as anxiety disorders, major depressive illness, or substance use disorder. Symptoms typically come on gradually, begin in young adulthood, and last a long time.

The causes of schizophrenia include environmental and genetic factors.

Panic attacks, depression, agoraphobia and anxiety disorders that I had appeared to conquer would perhaps have left me in the last stage of the journey toward becoming schizophrenic. Without help I very well could have been headed that way. With that in mind, so many people today diagnosed with schizophrenia do live normal lives and can function day to day very well with appropriate medications. If family and friends cannot be the main source of support, self-help books and support groups can be one of the greatest tools. This applies to anyone who on a smaller scale may just be suffering from insecurities, emotional hurts, or rejection. In other words, self-help books are for anyone who knows they are not perfect and are on a journey of hoping to be a better or more improved person tomorrow.

Because of all the books I had read, even during my struggles of being knee deep in my sickness, I was aware of the addictions that would inevitably add another disorder to my long list of problems. Although diazepam and lorazepam are the most prescribed in the valium or benzodiazepine families, it was my goal to use them not as a solution but as a means to get me to function enough in working through my healing. It kept me calm enough to stay on my vision of conquering these monstrous and crippling disorders so I could one day become established, strong and with a sound mind.

That brush with Dennis helped me to observe that I was approximately 80% on my way to a complete recovery.

I was getting married, I had two beautiful children, and I was off the prescription drugs. I was also doing well in the cosmetology school of training. Could things get any better?

For a while I was so busy in my world that I was getting more done in a day than most people would accomplish in two. I would forget that just brushing my teeth, washing a few dishes, changing a diaper, and putting on the television set was at one time the most I could do in a day. My fiancé did not see my past as a hindrance but rather to his credit focused on getting the prize which was me. With all the radar hunches in me and every womanly instinct and intuition, one thing I seemed sure of, no one had ever been so dedicated to win me over than this man. It was easy to surrender as all I wanted was to be loved.

The wedding day came and went. I had a new last name that was far more appealing than the one my last husband John left me with. For me the name Suzanne Mariani had a ring to it that felt like it would truly identify me for the rest of my life. As strange and humorous as this may sound my last names were just getting better and better! I was very disconnected to my birth name "Gendron." It was like wearing a garment with a loose fitting feel and I just wanted to shake it off.

BBC News magazine writer Carolyn McClatchey wrote (in part) October 18, 2011; "But there's a stage in most people's lives when they want to be something else, when they leave home or change jobs. It is a way of emancipating yourself from your past, particularly if you have unhappy associations."

A reasonable explanation in the assumption that, at least for me, the new name change had unexpectedly resulted in a perfect "fit like a glove " sensation, and it finally felt right. Like apples of gold!

We purchased a quaint little 840 square foot home in a small community that had many children, parks and schools. Since my husband adopted my two children, I was very dedicated to being a happy family and introducing those established and rooted French traditions that I remembered growing up with. However, my new husband was very European, and it essentially trumped my background to a solid inheritance of Italian culture. He was born on a boat in the middle of the ocean with no true location other than latitude and longitude   on his birth certificate. His parents were brave immigrants, leaving their families in Italy to venture forward to the land of opportunity called Canada, the true north strong and free!

Not a word of English left their lips. How could one not admire the passion and sacrifice of parents who daringly leave their countries for the sake of their children in the hope of offering them a better life?!

It was lunch every Sunday at Nonna's and Nonno's (Italian name for grandmother and grandfather).

Nonna's Italian cooking included lots of garlic, fresh tomatoes, peppers and basil from her home-grown garden. She was an incredible cook, and although I was not able to fully communicate in their language I was quietly eating and eating and eating, while the family was busy talking, talking and talking. "Mangiare," she would say, every time I walked in the door. It means "eat" in Italian. She would grab me by the waist and remind me I was terrifically thin. Her English was very broken, but the delivery in the way she threaded her thoughts into words was charming to say the least. If you left the kitchen table on a full stomach and complained about eating too much she would typically say, "Today is today, and tomorrow is tomorrow, so eat! Mangiare!"

20

Close Call

My husband was somewhat close to his siblings, something noteworthy to me as I did not experience that with my own. Other than my brother Paul I felt very estranged to the rest of my family growing up.

In the years of my living in the low income complex (the green houses), my brother Paul had moved back to Winnipeg after a hard life in Toronto, where he had become addicted to cocaine. He was a chronic user and the horror story of what he went through in withdrawals alone should have been enough to kill him. With great determination and the will to live, he has since been free from all recreational and euphoric drugs. He has suffered a heart attack and survived an aneurysm brain surgery.

Currently working in a full-time job as one of the top sales people in his workplace, I could not be more proud of him. He had the tenacity to triumph and to push through his darkest hours.

I am not bound to win, but I am bound to be true. I am not bound to succeed, but I am bound to live up to what light I have. —**Abraham Lincoln**

Once Paul moved back to Winnipeg we were together more often, and he would occasionally babysit for me and my husband.

Unfortunately, the marriage wasn't harmonious and I have learnt that when things are going well it's easy, but when they are not the commitment becomes frayed.

We were very busy with the two children and so there was little time to think about how unhappy I was. This was a saving grace in many ways.

If you can't fly then run, if you can't run then walk, if you can't walk then crawl, but whatever you do, you have to keep moving forward.
—**Martin Luther King**

Sometimes moving forward is all we can do instead of feeling sorry for ourselves, and to keep us in a composed "check."

Sadly, those feelings were on a priority list that sat on the bottom of the page, and I found myself aimlessly lashing out at my husband and my children. Still I ignored my paralyzing behavior with no thought of fixing it as that would mean dealing with sorrow again.

Although my husband faithfully adopted my children, he did desire to have his own biological and so I became pregnant with my third. This would undoubtedly keep me busy enough.

One day in the middle of the afternoon while in the first trimester of my pregnancy, I was feeling weak and tired, which caused me to lie down and rest. As mentioned in a previous chapter, I had lost a baby when I was approximately three months pregnant, and I was distressed it might happen to me again. I began to feel the cramping and a sudden burst of fluid left me, making my sheets wet, and I was back in the hospital miscarrying. I was hemorrhaging clots the size of a human liver but was unable to deliver the baby even with every effort from the hospital putting pressure on my stomach. I was approximately three or four months pregnant.

The idea of having a blood transfusion was in discussion just as it was with the last miscarriage. Since there was no miscarriage yet and I was losing too much blood they opted for a D&C (*dilation and curettage*), a surgical procedure in which the cervix is dilated and an instrument is used to scrape the uterine lining / to remove tissue in the uterus.

Lying in a cold room of sterile instruments and stainless steel tables I hear "count to ten backwards and you will be asleep by the time you get to one." Where had I heard that before? The surgeon was right, as a matter of fact, I didn't make my slumberous count to eight. Perhaps I was so exhausted with or without anesthesia that my droopy eyelids were screaming for unconsciousness.

When I opened my eyes I was ready to finish my countdown. Where was I, at the number seven? I thought. "We are all done, Mrs. Mariani. Get lots of rest as you lost a lot of blood." How did all that take place in less than a second? At least in the time zone of my comatose state I was completely unaware of anything that took place after my backwards count to eight.

At home lying in my bed I retreated back to that debilitated state of exhaustion, and fell into a deep sleep from which I could not wake up.

There are approximately 4 - 5 liters of blood in the body. Losing large amounts of blood quickly can lead to serious complications or even death. Severe blood loss is usually treated with a transfusion or medication. I had neither.

– A malfunction –

My body was drained, fatigued and giving way to the trauma. The blood loss was too much for my body to replenish properly, and it impaired my strength.

If the heart beats too slow and doesn't pump enough blood to meet the body's needs, death can be the life-threatening token waiting at the door.

As I recall I woke up in a panic and realized I was not even awake. I was trapped in an exhausted body that was too weak to move, to talk or to be awakened. My heart rate was so low that death was about to swallow me up. I could see a dark cloud shaped like a person holding a type of pillow and mercilessly making its way over my face to suffocate me. Since I was helpless and in a paralytic state I began to scream "Please, someone, wake me up!" "Jesus," I hollered over and over.

Who could hear me? I was trapped inside this motionless body and lost all power to make it yield to what I wanted it to do. Something I took for granted every day of my life. I could hear the sound of my own screams demanding my legs to move, anything to wake me up, but my body would not respond. I felt as if it had vacated and deserted me, leaving me in this isolated place where no one could hear me or find me.

A nightmare to say the least, yet I was awake enough to see it all from the inside. My spirit was alive, strong, and vibrant. There was no death for it. I could think, scream, talk, and reason, but it had nothing to do with my body anymore as that was shutting down. I was beginning to separate from it and the despondency of what was to me the "unknown" brought on much fear. It felt like a thief was stealing from me and I needed to take back what was mine.

I could feel my body trying to fight for a breath and I couldn't do anything about it but scream to Jesus one final time. "I don't want to die!" At that moment I felt hands under my back, and I was pushed off of my bed and onto the cold hardwood floor.

Oddly enough I recall the hands were warm and soft, and I felt their touch exuded safety.

With such a loud bang my husband ran into our bedroom to find out what the ruckus was. He was completely stunned that I had fallen out of bed. Something I had never done in my lifetime. "I just checked on you a minute ago," he says, "and you were sleeping like a dead log in the middle of the bed."

As I was unable to get up on my own from the floor, my husband picked me up and carried me to another room. I was too weak to walk and my body was steadily shaking. I asked my husband for a cigarette, and I sequentially smoked two or three. With the addition of a strong cup of caffeinated tea, my heart rate was accelerated and undoubtedly stimulated enough that I could feel a thrashing pulse transporting itself through my body.

How refreshing it was to finally feel a tranquil moment. The kids were sleeping soundly, and my husband was watching hockey while eating snacks and cheering on his favorite team in full volume. All seemed normal and I was shifted from fear to peace.

I reminded myself of the time when the semi was about to hit me at the age of seventeen and how miraculous it was that I was divinely plucked out in the exact moment the danger struck.

The warm and safe hands that had thrown me off my bed to kick-start my heart were the same ones that had safeguarded me that day. Not only is God omniscient (knowing all things) but he is promisingly omnipresent, being in all places at all times. He heard me while I was in the darkest pit of grief and terror where no light exists and no bottom can be found. One thing is for sure, God is never late!

A heathen philosopher once asked a Christian, "Where is God?" The Christian answered, "Let me first ask you, where is he not?"

21

Take Two

Many months had now come and gone and I was far too busy to reflect on any one thing. I would close my eyes at night and open them once again in the morning. Everything in between was about family, and laborious chores that would hopefully one day conquer a satisfying fulfillment of dividends earned. Then I could assuredly say with confidence that I'd raised good kids!

With this ongoing unhinged schedule I had not noticed that I had missed my monthly menstrual cycle. I was pregnant again!

If there was ever radar to depend on, then the heliograph's report on this one was that I had unquestionably decided that this pregnancy was a keeper.

On one particular quiet and soft toned day I was resting indoors and my husband was playing with the two kids outside on our front lawn. There was nothing really unusual, and actually it was for me a monotone day.

Without any warning I hear the screen door fly open, and there was my husband looking white as a sheet and bee-lining straight for me. "Suzanne, you're not going to believe this," he said. "I was playing ball with the kids and out of nowhere I heard God talk to me in my head. He told me to tell you that he is giving you twins to make up for the two miscarriages you've had." "No he did not!" I lashed out aggressively. "Why would God tell you something like that and not me?" I strongly stated my opinion on a quick reaction; however, inwards I felt sensitive to what he had just told me. There was this feeling of anger I had towards God. I believed that I was the one with the deeper and more spiritual side and yet God chose to speak to him and bypass me altogether. This was offensive to me and I made it known to my husband and then to God. Later in my reflecting further to this behavior of mine, I had realized I was somewhat puerile about it.

Several days had passed and I had already put this nonsense out of my mind. The phone rang, and it was my doctor's office calling me back to the clinic for another blood test. "Why?" I ask the nurse. "It appears your protein levels suggest you might be pregnant with a Down syndrome child," she says. "We will need to verify this result by administrating another blood test." My mind began to race and I startled myself as I impetuously recalled the conversation I had with my husband. "I dare ask, what if I was having twins? Would that affect my blood test in the same manner?" "Yes," she said, "that could be a possibility as well." I fell in my chair, astounded and taken aback. I wanted to run mad in a helter-skelter fashion to escape the confusion but sitting still to collect myself was all I could do for the moment.

An appointment for a second blood test and an ultrasound was scheduled. My husband, who asseverated he heard from God, insisted on accompanying me.

And so the day arrived where I lay comfortably on a hospital bed waiting for the ultrasound procedure to start. A cold, sticky and messy gel was applied to my belly and a probe of some sort glided carefully over my stomach area. All I saw on the monitor were fuzzy lines that I could not understand, and my husband was glued to that screen like it was a football game.

The ultrasound technician was not saying a word, but she seemed to be spending an awful lot of time scanning the same area on my tummy. I began to get a little concerned about this, and just as I was about to ask her if everything was ok, she blurted out "Congratulations, you are having twins!"

Perhaps now I could believe. It was so intangible at the beginning with a mere conversation of an idea or a thought, but it became a true prophetic word over my future, and this had to be a divine moment to embrace. And so we did.

During the pregnancy I had blood spotting, and thought another miscarriage was making its way to bring me despair once again. But those predictive words that I was having twins resonated back to me, and I knew a miscarriage would not happen.

I met with my gynecologist, who had concerns and ran many tests. The spotting was a result of abnormal cells in my cervix area, and unfortunately I had to wait till the twins were born and my afterbirth menstrual period stopped before I could get proper treatment. By then it could be full blown cancer cells.

A pap smear should be done annually for a woman. If abnormal cells are caught early enough the treatment of freezing them or burning them is the best option. If they are too far in advance a hysterectomy is the last option, or chemotherapy if the abnormal cells have escalated to cancer.

Although I was being tested monthly through my pregnancy to see how fast the abnormal cells were growing, gratefully it was not reaching the level of cancer. However, the number was climbing with every visit, and there was reason for concern.

I could have gone to bed every night wondering If I was going to die. The thought of not being able to get immediate treatment because I was pregnant was very disturbing, and yet I believed strongly in my heart it was not going to go in that direction.

I chose to live every day positively, and told myself I would enjoy my pregnancy. When you think you've heard from God that's a small mustard seed of faith that can grow into an "I know" I've heard from God and not an "I think" anymore.

That mindset carried me through my pregnancy and kept me content. I felt many times it saved me.

When the twins were two months old my gynecologist / specialist used the freezing method twice with no success. Our third attempt to destroy the abnormal cells would be the burning method, for which I had to be partially put to sleep. I was told if this method was not successful I would be having a hysterectomy.

The good news was that I did not need a hysterectomy. The burning of abnormal cells was successful.

Time went by quickly as I had no room to do anything outside of diapers, making lunches, attending school meetings, cleaning house, grocery shopping, running errands, planning meals, taking care of the household budget, getting kids to the doctor's office, and anything else that had to be done. I was on top of my game.

American astrophysicist, cosmologist, and science communicator Neil Degrasse Tyson once said "Being on the top of your game intellectually, philosophically, politically, is NOT a forever thing."

I suspect that this is a quote that won't clash with anything; it is unquestionably agreeable to all with certainty. It will never be considered for a dispute by anyone as we have all experienced a fall soon after we were on top of our game. No one ever stays there. Not the mountain climbers, the athletes, or The Beatles, Elvis Presley, Michael Jackson, Madonna, Elton John, Led Zeppelin or Pink Floyd. Just to name a few musicians "on top of their game" who have sold more than 250 million records. Their stories, and the stories of others, tell of the true climb and falls.

Mountains have peaks and valleys. It doesn't take long before we realize it goes down from there if there isn't another step to climb.

22

Scary Movie

Thinking I had it all together became a short season of self-reproach. "Busy" was an understatement in my world, as the window to find some "me" time was a non-existent one. Once I set my treadmill to the incline and speed I was comfortable surviving in, I continued the pace of my "on the go" assignment of life and didn't stop.

At some point my attention was deferred and my stride became sluggish. I noticed my oldest son appeared to be struggling in school and was escalating quickly in an unusual and odd behavior. Since he was four years old he had slight facial twitches, but within a few years it was intensifying to the point where his body had frequent involuntary movements. We enrolled him in hockey to give him an outlet to work off what we thought was restlessness, but when he was on the ice chasing the puck he would compulsively stop and jump a few times then continue to skate. None of us could understand this and unfortunately all I did was demean him for this. My past caught up with me, and I reacted to his deficiency to meet up with the "normal' expectation I had for him by yelling at him every time he came home from hockey or school. I recreated the house I grew up in. I was my mother, and my son was hurting the way I was when I was hit and yelled at as a child.

It wasn't long before this negative demeanor of mine overflowed onto all my children. I still hold tears about this, and on many occasions have asked my children to forgive me for all of my irrational conduct. I had allowed my past to slither back into my household. A responsibility I alone hold.

There was a long hard time when I kept far from me the remembrance of what I had thrown away when I was quite ignorant of its worth.
—**Charles Dickens,** *Great Expectations*

Exhausting all efforts to figure out my son's odd behavior, I decided to take him to our family pediatrician. Sitting in the doctor's office, my son played quietly, but instantaneously looked up at me in a puzzled manner when he heard the pediatrician say, "Your son seems very slow, and this is probably why he struggles in school. He will likely never do well and just isn't smart. "Not everyone is smart" he said. He most likely also has ADHD (Attention Deficit Hyperactivity Disorder). But that's ok," he announces loudly in his cold wintry bedside manner. Lots of kids are slow and have learning disabilities. He just happens to be one of them." "If you don't mind," I said abruptly, "you could have chosen your words more carefully. My son is right here, and one thing that is sharp about him is his hearing!"

I left that office with an undimmed understanding that I would never take my children to that practitioner again.

I recall in my mind so many times the expressions on every one of my children's faces when they were confused, afraid or disheartened. How they looked up at me for an answer, a hug, or a moment of security when they didn't understand something. They were so dependent on me for their safety and direction.

We as parents are our children's sanctuary. It is our undistracted obligation that legitimately belongs to them, and they have the right to own that from us!
—SM

I look back at how many times I blew them off because I was too busy and just plainly ignored them. How could I have been such a parent? Yet there was this other side of me that had an undeniable love that was so deep I would give up my life for them.

One of those "love days" was when I stormed out of that doctor's office. I was still steaming mad as I drove back home. My son, who was sitting in the passenger side of the car, mumbled, "Am I really stupid mom?"

My compassion barometer sky rocketed to high blood pressure levels. "You are so smart, son," I told him. "That doctor has no idea what he is talking about." Although my words and confidence temporarily soothed him, I could sense that those words from the pediatrician were seeded deeply within him. The kids were still teasing him at school, calling him "weirdo," and this only compounded more emotional insecurities for him.

I too began to second-guess myself about how I could react to this prognosis on my son, but my husband was adamant in reinforcing that this practitioner was undeniably wrong.

Running an errand one day, I ran into my old friend Darcie. I shared with her the frustration with my son's odd behavior, and that I could not understand why no one could figure out what seemed like what I called a "helter-skelter disorder." All those irksome involuntary movements and vocalizations were really mysterious to me, and downright creepy even. He would growl like a mad dog at times, and roll his eyes the same way I've seen in horror movies. I told Darcie we had to get him to wear a hockey jock to protect his groin as he would violently stab himself there with a fork when eating.

Running into her that day was beyond doubt a divine appointment that had to be. She mentioned I should see Doctor Rox Wand. "Who is that?" I asked her. "He is a psychiatrist who works with Tourette Syndrome patients. I'm thinking maybe this is what your son is suffering from," she said. Hearing this I couldn't wait to get home to do my research in diligence. I promptly gathered any supplementary information I could get my hands on regarding Tourette Syndrome.

I met with Doctor Wand, who determined that my son did suffer from this disorder. My friend was dead on! Dr. Wand referred to it as Gilles de la Tourette Syndrome.

In my further study of this disorder, I found information that was vague and yet inconclusive about a 1974 horror film called The Exorcist. Although there is no real proof, there are some who say the movie was based on a child who had Tourette Syndrome. Very strange indeed! "Is this just a fabricated myth?" I thought. "Fiction or non-fiction?"

One thing was for certain, when I stumbled on this information I remembered a moment that took place years ago when I was pregnant with my son. I watched The Exorcist. In 1999 Entertainment Weekly named it the scariest movie of all time, and it probably still is today.

According to several sources, several deaths and near deaths were associated with the filming of The Exorcist.

Televangelist Billy Graham stated, "There is a power of evil in the film, in the fabric of the film itself."

One evening, I was flipping through the television channels and there was a horrific scene of a young girl possessed by a demon. Her eyes were rolling back and then she spun her head around 360 degrees. It seemed so overbearing to watch and yet it was jumping out of the television set like it was screaming "Don't touch that dial!" so I didn't. I was on the edge of my seat, feeling terror, but couldn't get myself to change the channel. Although this took place many years ago I remember I was in my parents' living room. They had two separate sofas to choose from. My father was laying on one of them, drunk and fast asleep, and I was on the other. My mother was out and my daughter was fast asleep in another room.

A sudden noise came out of my father and he began to mumble words I had never heard before. He was acting strange and the murmurings were getting louder and louder. He startled me as he was acting as though he was having spasmodic convulsions. His eyes were fixed shut but they were moving vigorously under his eyelids.

I was so petrified I jumped off the sofa and screamed at my father to wake up. All this was taking place simultaneously when the possessed little girl in the movie was manifesting her head spinning and flying across the room in diabolical ways. Once my father was awake I was calmer, and without hesitation I shut the television set off. He had no recollection of anything and expressed to me his bold disbelief. For many nights following I slept with the lights on as I was steadily consumed with fear. With some discernment I've come to interpret this as a demonic influence. I believe this comes through by invitation, meaning allowing fear of this type to be in front of us and not shutting it down as we should.

I've learned that horror movies attract a different energy in our space, that I truly believe can be mind-altering.

23

Taken Over

With my French background I found it interesting that George Gilles de la Tourette was a French physician who was renowned for his continued work on hypnotism, hysteria, and neurological conditions. The French origin of the disorder is La Maladie de Gille de la Tourette. Today he would have been classified as a neurologist, although the field did not exist in his time.

Tourette Canada describes it this way: Tourette Syndrome or TS is a neuropsychiatric or brain-based condition that causes people who have it to make involuntary sounds and movements called tics.

Wikipedia notes that Tourette described the symptoms as "maladie des tics." It recounts that a contemporary neurologist by the name of Jean Martin Charcot renamed the syndrome "Gilles de la Tourette" in his honor.

The Tourette Association of America states the following: *Tragically in 1893, both Gilles de la Tourette's son and his mentor Jean-Martin Charcot died. During that very same year, Gilles de la Tourette was shot in the head, but not killed, by an apparently psychotic woman (Rose Kamper) who claimed that she had been hypnotized at the*

Salpêtrière hospital and was now incapable of making a living. Ironically, Gilles de la Tourette himself later developed psychiatric (probably depression and dementia) and neurological (neurosyphilis) illnesses and, in 1901-1902, he was forced to leave his hospital appointment and was admitted to a hospital for mental illnesses in Lausanne, Switzerland. His condition deteriorated significantly and shortly thereafter he died on May 22, 1904.

Although what my son was going through was trying on him, it was also weight-bearing on all family members. We did, however, find ourselves relieved to know what we were dealing with actually had a name associated to it, and most of the ambiguity was no longer a provocation to deal with. Unfortunately, he had TS and was demon possessed. *Double whammy!*

One afternoon The Tourette Society showed a film at the school for all students and teachers. It was located in the school gym and all for the benefit of my son in helping others understand the behavior of those who suffer with TS, and about its origin. Although there was much material available to learn, there was never enough for me, and so I looked forward to the afternoon film to continue my education regarding this disorder.

It was a very enlightening film and you could hear a pin drop if there was one to drop. The students were so fascinated and all eyes were fixed on the show.

In a short video characterizing TS, William Shatner says, *"It is uncontrollable movements and sounds. Symptoms include fast eye blinks, facial grimaces, jerking of the head or shoulders. Uncontrollable noises include grunting, barking sniffling, and involuntary use of words. It's frustrating when your body does something you don't want it to."*

With my son the symptoms also tended to fluctuate. This is not uncommon. There would be facial twitching for a short time, then a new tic would surface like swinging his arms when they were just resting at his sides. We would adapt to one of his tics, and then a new one would rise up and the old one was gone.

He was very good at hiding his twitches at family gatherings. Once we all got into the car he would yelp, holler strange words and burst out in animal sounds. From the time we walked in the door he would make his way to his room and stay there for a while just to tic. It was a relief to him, since he had been holding it in for several hours. Eventually he was no longer able to keep this under control and he was put on a pharmaceutical treatment called Haloperidol (Haldol) which made him extremely drowsy. This was frustrating as it affected his attentiveness in school and he was unable to concentrate properly when it came to homework.

During the film in the school gym that day I recall the narrator sharing that many people in centuries past would be burnt to the stakes if they were considered to be demonized. The Catholic Church was successful at times by using a spiritual deliverance method called an exorcism. The film did share the pre-eminent lack of knowledge of the accusers, who were confused about whether people who had involuntary movements and vocalizations were in fact demon possessed. It was an easy fix to burn them to the stake as their behavior was abnormal to society, and these involuntary actions did not match up to any of their current mainstream science. They had to justify their conclusions. Research or medical opinions were not in the path of influence in those early centuries.

However, any person who has Tourette Syndrome, or anyone with a related neurological disorder will determine it has its own unique characteristics. And those characteristics will manifest differently for each person. Shortly after watching the film, I decided that my son was indeed possessed. This resulted from my interpretation of a series of strange events. My son was found crying one night and hitting himself, screaming "I want to be normal, I want to be normal!" He was frustrated that he couldn't stop hitting himself. My husband and I grabbed him out of his bed, and I placed him on my lap in a rocking chair, where he hollered, growled, and was so strong that we were not able to hold his arm down. We allowed him to hit himself in the groin till his arm finally gave way and fell to his side. Thank goodness we had a jock for him to wear as this was his fundamental common tic.

As long as I live I will never forget the emotion and empathy I had for my son. I wanted to give him the world, to bring him peace and to save him from the ostracized and unjust world he was living in. I had nothing to offer him but to hold him on that somber and grimy night. Streams of tears flowed down my cheeks and I felt helpless for not having any power of my own to solve his unending torment.

In an earlier chapter I shared how my life was miraculously spared on a bridge where I should have died. Instead I was supernaturally removed from the scene, in a way that no theorist or science could rationalize. I amused myself and thought, "If God is real and he saved me that day on the bridge, then it's time I find out how real he is."

So I decided to pray. I was on my knees with my hands clasped together, and my words were, "God, I need you to show me what I can do for my son." That was it. I got up and went about my usual business.

– I can do this –

A few days went by and I kept getting a buffeting nudge to open my Bible. As I scrambled through its pages, I found myself going through the New Testament chapters of Mark, Luke, and Matthew. There I found an interesting story of a little boy who was possessed by demons, and none of the disciples were able to deliver him. Jesus looked at them and said *"You faithless generation" this one only comes out with fasting and praying!* He called the disciples faithless? I was relentless with passion to help my son, and I knew what I had to do. I decided to fast, and reminded myself I was not going to be faithless.

When reading further I read that Jesus also called that demon by name. He said, "You deaf and dumb spirit, come out of him." Whatever that meant! Some intuition on the inside of me told me my son had this same demon.

Benjamin Franklin once said "Work as if you were to live a hundred years, pray as if you were to die tomorrow."

I was on a mission and all this knowledge came from that small prayer. "God, show me!"

My son came home from school one day and he was ticking like mad. There was no time to take off his boots or winter coat; he was hitting himself and yelping uncontrollably. I looked right at him and said out loud like a crazy woman, "You deaf and dumb spirit, get out of him!" By the time I said that, my son had elevated from the ground a few feet and was thrown against the door he was standing by. It was like a strong wind blew him there. I was both freaked out and amazed at the same time. My son was abruptly dropped to the ground and then removed his boots and coat like nothing unusual had just happened. By dinner time he was at it again, and behaving exceedingly worse. He was growling and rolling his eyes, and I became frightened. He eventually began to convulse as though he was having a seizure, and I had to rush him to the hospital.

When we arrived, there wasn't an intern in that cold and gloomy emergency room that didn't tactfully request to be the examiner of my son. I remember hearing some of the medical staff having a profound "groupthink" of figuring that one out. Since having a severe Tourette Syndrome patient was not the norm in their emergency room, it was nonetheless an outright flamboyant show for them.

We were there for hours, but sadly enough they had very little relief to offer him for his extreme and relentless ticking that day. However, we were thrilled that the convulsing had stopped on the way to the hospital. They offered no advice due to the perplexity of this disorder, as they were just as dumbfounded as we were.

This is by no means a judgment or critique, as twenty-five years ago less information was available on this disorder. Furthermore, much of the reading material for the medical profession was not always up to date, sometimes slow moving, sometimes fast moving. Tourette Syndrome was then, and still is, a fairly rare and unique disorder, and education is vital. There is much learning still to be done.

24

An Exorcism

There are far too many details, events, and occurrences that took place, and to detail them all "au courant "would be a book in itself. However, the story ultimately and finally leads to a path of integral freedom for my son.

An exorcism was performed.

__As a disclaimer;__ I am not suggesting that anyone with Tourette Syndrome is demon-possessed. This is my true story of events in my situation, and does not reflect on any other person or persons with a similar disorder.

With countless demonic symptoms manifesting themselves through my son, it was obvious to me they were more than straightforward Tourette Syndrome tics or verbal outbreaks.

I knew the day would come when I would decide to test my faith in this area, and be ready to face this monster tormenting my son. I opened my Bible to *Matthew 17:18-20. "Jesus rebuked the demon, and it came out of the boy, and he was healed at that moment. Afterward the disciples came to Jesus privately and asked, "Why couldn't we drive it out?" "Because you have so little faith," Jesus said. "Truly I tell you, if you have faith as small as a mustard seed, you can say to this mountain, 'Move from here to there,' and it will move. Nothing will be impossible for you."*

But here was the "coup de grâce" for me, the culminating factor that bound my action to remove this demon. I touched on this in the previous chapter, when I mentioned that Jesus said " However, this kind does not go out except by prayer and fasting."

I had a conversation with God months prior, stating that fasting wasn't my thing, and I was far too much of a "Type A" personality, with a high energy disposition, to be able to go without food for long periods of time. With four kids and a husband who needed my undivided attention, I just couldn't see myself giving up physical stamina and possibly go anemic on my family. I could not understand where the benefit would be in my weakness by living on water when I needed energy. What was God thinking when he said this? How could people get through the day on water only?

Although I was not able to discern the true meaning of fasting at that time, I was able to take a baby step, where I pledged to God that one meal a day I would replace with one cup of water. And so it was every noon hour for many months.

With a strong conviction in my heart, one night it came to me that this would be my last day of fasting. The kids had all gone to bed and my husband was out picking up a few things I needed at the grocery store. The hour was late, but I heard my son get out of bed while I was sitting quietly in the living room. I quickly glanced over as he walked out, and in an almost muted tone he said "Mom, I'm just going to the washroom." He was quiet and calm, but within a few minutes the yelping and verbal outbreaks and tics were getting the best of him. "Come here," I said. "I think it's time for you to be free of this, so we are going to pray together. Would you like that?" He immediately said "Yes mom, (tic), (verbal outbreak), I just want (tic), (verbal outbreak) to be like the kids at school." (tic), (verbal outbreak)

I explained to my son that "When I pray out loud, something inside of you will not like it and you may feel divided. But don't worry. Find yourself and remember the part that doesn't like it is really not you." I went on to say, "God promises us that he never takes away our own will. So when I start to pray, concentrate on what I am saying, and remember your will belongs to you only! Let's trust God."

Just before I started to pray I remembered the verse I read that day in Luke 9:20, about the little boy who was demon possessed. As the boy came forward, the demon knocked him to the ground and threw him into a violent convulsion. But Jesus rebuked the evil spirit and healed the boy. Then he gave him back to his father.

With some of the horror movies I had watched over the years I was petrified that this type of hair-raising scene might materialize in front of me if I did this. I remembered that the priest had died in the end of the movie The Exorcist. He tried to rebuke the demon and he ended up dead, which was not an outcome I wanted. I felt terror-stricken just thinking about it. Although it was just a movie, there were a few spiritual truths found in it regarding the laws of the spiritual realm.

The law of gravity is in motion whether we believe it or not. The spiritual realm is also in motion and it too follows its own order. No human or science can reverse, change, or alter its course. It remains intangible and adheres to the decree and statute of true ownership that "IT IS" and will never change its rules or truism. —SM

However, I had gone this far in the path and I truly believed that all the signals and wonders were adding up to one thing. I was either a fool or God was real.

To set the stage, we were both sitting comfortably on the living room floor. My son was sitting in a crossed-leg position looking up at me, and I knelt beside him in a praying of hands position. This was not necessary, but it was my way of being humble before God.

I thanked God for the freeing moment my son was about to experience. I believed with all my heart the evidence of an incredible power had engaged this session for a "tête-à-tête" (one on one).

I immediately admonished the deaf and dumb spirit to get out of my son. It was short and sweet. Not one but many demons came out non-violently. They exited out of every opening of his body except his ears. I had boldly declared to them that they must leave quietly, and they yielded to that request. Without a tremble or a waver they surrendered. It was unbelievable, crazy, fantastic, supernatural, but mostly freeing and liberating!

However, something very unusual was hanging out of my son's nose so I grabbed a tissue and it slithered out. It was long, thick and felt like a parasite to the touch. I recall standing in front of my kitchen garbage completely mesmerized and benumbed. I could not stop staring at it, as it was like nothing I'd ever seen before. And it appeared lifeless. All of a sudden I heard a subtle yet resounding voice in my head, and it startled me.

"While you're busy gazing on that which is in the tissue, your eyes are off of me. Throw it away and focus on what is true, lovely and noble. The healing of your son is from me."

It was a clear, crisp sentence that flowed out like milk and honey. I knew it had to be God, as I would not have thought of it myself while looking at that ugly, diabolic leech.

I had not realized I had cloaked my mind with a veil of negative thoughts that were distracting me from the real focus, which was the victory!

This was such a grand slam victory that my son was running back and forth in our little 840 square foot bungalow in disbelief and in awe at the same time. He went from one door to the next to grab on to each door handle with the intention of turning it, and was in "wonderment" that they actually opened on the first try. "Wow," was all he could say as he sprinted from one door to the next. This was something he could never do before. His tics would usually take over, swaying his hand off the handle, and so it would take many attempts to be steady enough to follow through the full turn.

My husband, unaware of what had just happened in our home, walked in the front door to have all this good news flung at him! Strangely enough, he was calm. Because I had talked about this with him for so long, he knew the day was coming and was very supportive.

So my son went off to school the next day with no more tics! At approximately 2pm, I received a phone call from one of the teachers requesting I meet her and a few more teachers to discuss this new prevailing "normal" behavior of my son. She seemed cynical and made me feel as though we had put on a false show and that I had some explaining to do. I felt chastised. "How could this be?" she asked. She then insisted that we meet at 3:45 in the school conference room that afternoon.

25

Point Blank

I rushed to the school but I felt nauseous. When I got off the phone with the "snippety" teacher it made me feel like I just got kicked in the stomach. How could I be so happy one minute and then have opposing feelings the next? I felt discouraged, not having a more positive reaction from the school. What would they think of me? Would they call the children's welfare agency when I told them I performed an exorcism on my son? The thoughts were racing through my mind as I desperately tried to figure how I would rationalize this without coming across like a lunatic.

British poet Alfred Tennyson once said, "Once in a golden hour, I cast to earth a seed. Up there came a flower, the people said a weed."

Just as I pressed the bar of the school's grand double doors, a wind of fear pressed up against my body. It made me hesitant to walk through. My heart was racing, and the tightening in my chest was so severe that I had to stop. I leaned up against the wall closest to me, then looked up as though there was an answer in the heavens. I seized the moment to capture for myself a long and drawn out breath.

I had a jump on stress long before I left the house, and now I had to face the music of how to tell this story to an assembly of folded-armed educators prudently waiting for my grand entrance.

Prior to leaving the house I remember thinking "What am I going to say?" A voice in my head darted through my thoughts like a flash of lightning, and I heard "Don't worry, once you get there I will give you the words." There was now no doubt that the still small voice inside of me had to be a celestial sign from God, that he would get the right words out of my mouth in perfect time.

The moment ceased as I entered the room. Three people were sitting close to each other at an oversized long, oblong, boardroom-style table. It was awkwardly intimidating, as there were many empty chairs to choose from. I select an unoccupied one that was away from the table, opposite where the educators huddled together.

Without anyone saying a word I blurted out, "Have any of you seen the movie The Exorcist?"

No response. It was like the timer shut off on the stop watch. I couldn't believe the frozen look on their faces. Their jaw-drop reactions were all in sync as their eyes glared at me with shock and disparagement. It took a few seconds for them to process the answer to that question. They pondered on it as though it was a riddle. "Yes" they all said simultaneously. "We have seen the movie."

"Good!" I said. "Same scenario here, but the priest lives." It didn't take much for them to figure out that in the movie the priest dies trying to remove the demon, but in my scenario the priest happened to be me, and I lived.

That was it! No drama, no chaos, no confusion. One of the teachers became emotional and said "I always believed these kinds of things could happen, and I am very happy for your son and what you've done. Her eyes were teary, while the other two were still in the frozen section of their mind, trying to figure out what just happened here. However, it was irrelevant to me as I remembered God had said, "I will give you the words." And he did.

We moved forward every day with the new adjustments to no more demonic growls, manifestations, tics, hollering or yelping in the house. There was also no rebellion left in him. My son, who was not able to write properly without scribbling, ultimately became student body president of the college he attended. Today he is self-employed, and is married to a young, new, and upcoming litigation lawyer. I couldn't be more proud!

If everyone is moving forward together then success takes care of itself. —**Henry Ford**

Looking back, some of the victories that exuded the most sublime joy had many more failures to come. Shortly after my son's healing, my marriage fell apart. Our goals, our dreams and communication became short-lived. There had never been any discussion between us of building a future together. As a result, when the well became dry there was no thirst left in us to be together. We lived in the same house but we were undoubtedly mentally divorcing ourselves from each other.

At the time I had a small aesthetic business I was running out of my home, with many clients round the clock scheduling facials, makeup, manicures and leg waxing. When the twins were babies, it was difficult for me to sustain my self-employment, as my customers were beginning to complain when the babies were crying in the middle of one of their treatments. Although it was unprofessional on my part, many of my loyal customers were willing to put up with the interferences. They were all-embracing to hang in there with me in the long term, being pleased with the results of my services.

Unfortunately, I was unable to keep up as I became discouraged and in all probability suffered postpartum depression. Something few people talked about back then. "Get over it; you're not the only one who's had babies" was my parents' and their parents' generational motto to keep moving forward.

Ultimately I yielded to the feelings of sadness, and sold most of my equipment and inventory to another professional aesthetician. I no longer felt capable of juggling schedules, and needed to lighten the load.

No fault to my husband, but the timing of his choice in changing careers was an added stress in my mind, and our relationship eventually spiraled downward like we were in bloodthirsty quicksand.

Money was scarce, and we had to do something impetuous. I will never forget the fear that crawled through my skin as my thoughts regressed back to where I use to be. Without dreams or hopes!

– Impoverished –

One morning after looking at our bare cupboards I picked up the phone to dial 411 (directory assistance) I asked the operator for food bank locations in the city. I chose one downtown where all patrons were given a shopping bag at the main door entrance of this non-profit facility. I lined up uniformly with others, to receive items of food from separate stations. I couldn't help but notice the persons in front of me and the persons behind me seemed to be receiving handfuls of food items, while I was given only one item per station. I could feel the eyes of judgment on me from the borders of both sides. The volunteers and those standing in line with me exuded an apprehension about me, suggesting I did not belong. The heaviness of their discrimination weighed on my heart.

The following week we were back in the same situation, and I was determined to find another non-profit food bank that would not endeavor to segregate me. I was becoming very isolated, and had grievously journeyed back into an introversion of not expressing to anyone how I truly felt. I had quarantined my feelings into believing that I had become a failure and no one could ever be proud of me. "I am worthless." And yet, I clung to the one thing in front of me, food for my children! And so I determined to make my way to a new food bank location.

Every woman that finally figured out her worth has picked up her suitcases of pride and boarded a flight to freedom, which landed in the valley of change.
—Shannon L. Alde

26

Bitter Pill

Finally the fog became clear!

With a little search I found a new food shelter location, which was organized by the neighboring community in a nearby church only a few blocks from my house. "Perfect!" I thought. It was a landslide getting in and out of there. I had a skip in my step and an old nursery rhyme in my head. "Baa baa black sheep, have you any wool? (I mean food.) Yes sir, yes sir, three bags full!"

The front of the church had two large, magnificent architectural double doors that were approximately 9-10 feet in height. It had an awe-inspiring sensation whether you were just admiring them, or walking through them.

With both arms straight down and by my side, the weight of the food bags was stretching like an elastic band, gravitating downwards, and I thought for sure they would give way and tear. I made my way through the grandiose doors, but just as I stepped outside I saw a vehicle drive by that I recognized. "Oh no, it's my neighbor." An alarm went off in my head. "Run, you can't let him see you!"

In a panic, my legs bounced like a spring, and I dashed behind the beautifully trimmed hedges only a few feet away. Bent down and on my knees I was well hidden. I discreetly moved the branches on both sides to create a microscopic eye view as I watched my neighbor's truck drive by. The coast was clear, and I was certain he did not see me. Like looking in the mirror, I realized that I was a full-grown woman who foolishly reacted and hid behind a bush because of shame. This visceral reflex had quickened my emotion and bypassed my intellect.

Failing is not a disgrace unless you make it the last chapter of your book. —**Jack Hyles**

As my heart rate became calm, I saw myself for what I was, and I broke down in an eruption of tears. In no sight of anyone, I dropped my head to rest on my knees and cried till exhaustion. Half an hour went by, and it was time to wipe off the soil that had statically clung to my skin. I made my way to our family car and was abruptly inspired with a thought. As I inserted the key into the ignition I looked straight ahead and said out loud "I will NEVER beg for food again!"

Progress lies not in enhancing what is, but in advancing toward what will be. —**Khalil Gibran**

It was a light bulb moment on my way home that I just believed I would never line up for food again. How did I know this? The experience was devastating for me and I had no idea, no clue, and no perception that things could ever change until I proclaimed it and believed it that day. Determined and passionate about NOT standing in a food line ever again became my "axe to grind" steering wheel, for where I was about to go.

I had drawn this line in my mind and it was like I never knew I was armed or equipped to change my circumstances. It was like a secret prodigy lurking around me that I didn't know existed within me. But when the words "that's enough" snapped in me," the trajectory of my thinking chased every indecisive and wavering thought right out of my mind.

You never know how strong you are until being strong is your only choice. —**Bob Marley**

Days went by and we still had food in the house. We had scraped by without going to a food bank.

Decision one was accomplished. Now on to decision two. The marriage was noticeably dissolving, and I determinedly went forward to start divorce proceedings. This was not an easy choice. And with my Christian faith it was without doubt spiritually conflicting. I knew that God hated divorce, with its heart-rending ramifications in the breaking up of families. I didn't want to disappoint him and I did understand that children need their fathers. With all the Christian counseling we did, there was still no progress in our communication, and I felt I was living with a stranger who never understood me. The silent treatments between us were trying for both of us. I was dying a slow death, surrounded in loneliness, and drowning in the turmoil of confusion.

Making the decision to leave my husband came with a hefty price tag. I was firmly chastised by some of our mutual friends, and this was a reaction I did not expect. The kindness and warmth I once experienced with some of them was quickly dissolved by one single shift I made. I was now doomed by them and was rendered a sentence of their unredeemable judgment. They took umbrage with me and never communicated with me again.

"Que sera sera, whatever will be will be!" I thought.

A friend that flips on a coin and doesn't stick with you during the bad and ugly times is simply not a friend.
—SM

Being insecure most of my life, I did surprise myself at times by "standing tall" when I needed to. And each time I did, another cup of unrestrained self-esteem was poured back into me. There is also something to be said about someone who comes to the end of their rope.

— Courage rises up and an action is soon to take place —

I remember lying in my bed at night thinking I was next to a man who was more like my brother or an acquaintance, we were so far apart. My faith as a Christian was holding me back from leaving him, until one night I had a dream that changed everything.

I dreamt my thirteen year old daughter was now a full-grown woman, and married. She was not getting along with her husband, as he was saying things that were hurtful to her and she didn't know what to do anymore. In this dream they had gone to many counseling sessions but nothing worked. One day my daughter ran into my house and lunged into my arms. It was like she had regressed to being five years old and would not let go of her mother. She held me tight and cried convulsively in my arms while unraveling words from her broken heart. Suddenly there was a knock on the front door and we could see through the grilled window it was her husband. "Mrs. Mariani," speaking to me directly, through the door, "please let me in so I can explain our situation. Your daughter's tears are not really genuine, and there are two sides of the story here. Please let me in and hear me out." He continued, "She too has faulted in our marriage."

Hearing this, my daughter was troubled that I might open the door and he would have his opportunity to persuade me. In my dream he had a calm eloquence about him, and her fear was that she would lose my support. "Please mom," she said, as tears continued to flow down her cheeks, "do not open the door." She wanted my full attention.

Suddenly a deep compassion fell on my heart, as I listened to my daughter and not her husband. I did what any mother or father would do. I stood with her. I reminded him he had his own family to run to, and so he left the front steps of my house. I quickly wrapped my daughter in a cloak (manteau) and hugged her tightly. I was compelled to make her feel safe, warm and secure. I could not squeeze her in enough, trying to make the pain go away for her. I realized even in my dream it was about finding the true love of being able to cry on the shoulders of someone you can trust. I woke up right there (tout de suite), sat straight up in my bed very overwhelmed and bewildered. It felt so real. Still in the trance of my thoughts I heard a voice in my head that said "How much more do I love you?"

It was God conferring with me through a dream to grant me understanding. He continued, "Run to me, have no concern of what anyone thinks. Run to me, I am your father and your true advocate. Run to me, where wisdom is found. Run to me, I am your support. Run to me, Run to me!"

Confidence was now at my door. By noon I had called a lawyer, set up the appointment, and my husband was served divorce papers one week later. We became much angrier with one another as each day passed, and before I knew it we were both filled with hatred and bitterness.

Where was God? At night I now lay in my bed alone, filled with anxiety and looking up at the ceiling, unable to sleep.

In my confusion, I kept circulating the same questions over and over in my mind. Was I in the wrong in our marriage? Or was it him? My husband and I both had plenty to say about it. Yet with all the befuddle puzzlement in my life, the words "run to me" would once again make their grand entrance into my heart.

Every time those words gathered in me I would instantly conceal them. I would run with them, and run to him. It was a "let go and let God" moment. When I did that I was able to leave it on his shelf to deal with.

I found myself broke and in debt. I became bitter towards my husband for quitting his job, and earmarked him as the entire blame. I forgot everything I had learned early on about moving forward. I just couldn't do it this time. I felt resentment towards him, and was too angry to think about forgiving him or looking at myself in the mirror. So here I was back in an old familiar space of being alone and afraid.

My husband moved out grudgingly as he was forced out by my declaration that our marriage was unchangeably over. If I was ever sure about anything at that time, it was without doubt ending this marriage.

It would cost me to stay and it would cost me to leave. I chose the latter.

27

Pursuit

Like any parent, you hang in there with your kids when they go through miserable times. Both his father and mother, who are very nurturing people, didn't think twice about having my husband stay with them for a while till he figured things out.

For me it was a whole new audacious quest! I remained in that house till the bank repossessed it. We were also behind in our property taxes, and that was the crowning blow that set us miles back.

Time was running out, and so the house was reclaimed by the bank.

Back to the day after my husband moved out, I decided to go out and buy a few cans of paint. The kids and I began to paint the walls to refresh the house. It was very therapeutic, and we finished off the night with pizza. I did everything I could to keep things as normal as possible, If there was such a thing.

However, I broke that normalcy when I shared with my children too much, and rebutted to them every time my husband mentioned something to the kids that I did not feel was accurate or if I did not agree. There was plenty of anger.

The back and forth fighting ended up causing our kids to be in the middle of it. No one was exempt from the heinous wounds. The children were innocent, and the only two responsible for the weight placed on them were their parents.

There are two sides to every story as long as there are two involved. —SM

I had a friend who cleaned houses for a living, and in an ironic timing of her busy season she was overloaded with customers, and so she asked me if I could help her. "Yes, yes and yes," I told her. "When can I start?"

Cleaning homes was a quick cash grab to help pay my bills and to put some food on the table. I became a pretty handy person around the house and fixed many things on my own, even though it was just a matter of time before the bank would repossess it. It was an immediate cash flow now, and I was able to pay the monthly mortgage. But I was still financially hog-tied to pay the arrears of taxes owed, and the bank refused to negotiate a smaller payment in order to reverse the foreclosure proceedings. It was a very fulminated and aggressive statement that read, PAYMENT IN FULL ONLY!

– It's my sugar –

Listening to music, singing out loud, painting all the walls and fixing things that needed repair was really not necessary to do, seeing that, in due time, the day was coming when I would be thrown out of this lovely property we all called home!

"Mom, please stop singing," the kids would plead. "Mother, are you done singing?" I remember one day practicing vocalization techniques for nine hours. It was so therapeutic for me to sing, to clean, and to fix anything that was broken (except my marriage).

I couldn't fix that anymore, and I was exhausted trying. And so my heart became an empty and vacant cavern yearning to be filled. A mental picture would leap into my thoughts of when I was a little girl, when my imagination travelled to where my dreams of "clouds and wonders" resided. Where I would lock myself in my room to play music, sing out loud, and dance solitarily.

The dream of that little girl brewed up in me once again, and the desire to sing was now stronger than ever. Of course I had no idea how to sing. I was terrible at it and without doubt off key more than you can imagine. It was a tormenting screech to anyone who dared to listen. Sadly, my children reaped the brunt of that noise pushing out of my mouth day and night. I remember one of my twins petitioned to have everyone get a set of ear plugs, he was so "thumbs down" about it.

I was completely blinded to their annoyance with me, as I was too busy immersing myself in a passion that overtook me. What they didn't know was that I felt I had lost my pulse. I just didn't feel alive anymore. The load of providing for my children alone and losing our home with no place to go was too much to bear and, ultimately, it simply hurt to live.

Singing became a quick form of healing, and put life back into my bones. Like fire in the belly!

There are no eloquent words spoken in any language to characterize enough how provocative it is when something puts breath back into you. —SM

It was like a calling, a door I had to walk through; I was raptured by it and it was like an artery attached to my heart. No way of separating it, it just had to be. And so it steered me in a direction that would inevitably help to change the course of my life.

I have learned that most dreams are so mortally out of reach when they first introduce themselves to us that we generally just brush them off. We assume they are too unattainable at the moment. "How do I get there?" we ask ourselves. The answer is "I don't know" and so we push the dream away.

When we truly understand the dream in us, we realize the dream is nothing more than a true gentleman. It stands at the door of your heart and knocks. It does not force itself upon you, but rather reminds you while your head is deep in the sand that you can take your dream, pull it out, and breathe again. Complex because you're not there yet, simple because when you get there you will say that you fully understood the spoor of faith it took in your baby steps to make the dream alive. And so it unveils itself and is in union with you. No longer does it knock at your door waiting to get in. "My dream," you will say, "is alive and living well in me!"

It wasn't long before it was rumored that all I did was sing around the house 24/7. In fact I wasn't dreaming of getting on any big stage; it started with just trying to stay on key. You have to do the one thing you know you are capable of doing next. Baby steps!

People too weak to follow their own dreams will always find a way to discourage yours. —**Oprah**

With an overwhelming reality I realized that some family members, acquaintances, and key friends, who I thought were supportive of me, were trying to tell me who I should and should not be. "That I should not search out what will never be." "You're not a good singer," they would say. "You really should not be wasting your time on this." Hearing those compounding and repeating statements of "no if ands or buts" undoubtedly impacted me. I was crushed by the echoing words and what they represented to me. My head was back in the sand.

28

Bats In The Belfry

Realizing that my odd housecleaning jobs weren't in consonance with my future, I knew that I would have to find a more lucrative occupation, now that I was the main bread-winner for my children. My husband didn't find work right away, but I geared up for court proceedings anyway, to settle our separation agreement in the hopes of wrapping up with a divorce decree.

I thought, since we didn't own much, it would be a slam dunk. I would be divorced and just move on with my life.

Sadly, there was so much anger between us that it ended up being approximately a two-year court battle of nothings. He had financial legal assistance on his side, but I couldn't afford a lawyer any longer and so I decided to represent myself. I didn't qualify for legal aid with the new job.

I had picked up the Saturday morning paper one day to read the classifieds ads. Lo and behold, a beauty supply company was looking for a salesperson to promote their professional products to salons throughout the city. "Just my thing," I thought, "makeup, professional hair products and accessories, organizing hair color classes for hairstylists and traveling to other countries for major hair shows. Wow, this is for me!"

I applied and they hired me on the spot. It was one of those "ma and pa" operations but I loved it. It put me back in my confidence mode, and I believed once again that I could do anything. If I wanted to make money I just had to go out and sell! It turned out that it was not that easy! However, I had the drive, and I was desperate for a full-time job. The owners were an older couple who were living proof that opposites do attract. The wife had a strong and unshakable stubborn personality, yet fair in all her conclusions. She was a "Ma Kettle" who knew how to hold the fort down for her brood of chicks. The husband was like moldable Jell-O and conformed well in any situation. He was passive and always accommodating. Everyone loved his upbeat and charismatic nature.

I met with the wife first. Once I passed first base of impressing her, I was off to bring down the curtain of the next part of the interview with her husband. "I will hire you," he said. "I thank you for your honesty," he continued. "Your home situation sounds like you've got a big load to bear, especially trying to keep up with feeding all those kids and putting a roof over their heads. I am deeply moved by your persistence and I feel you will be a good fit in our company. Can you start tomorrow?" "I can start today," I said with a chuckle.

The day was finally over, and I sat in my favorite golden oak and black leather gliding chair. I grabbed one of my cushions and held it tight against my stomach, in the hopes it could make me feel warm, safe and secure. "In less than a month the bank will be changing the locks of my house and this will never be our home again" were the words in my head that I suckled to.

Feeling sorry for myself and wallowing in my sorrows set me back an hour before I snapped out of that "I'm an injured party" mindset. Wiping away my tears, I pulled out my note pad and begin to skim over my notes under the heading "bucket list."

No. 1 - A full-time job. I crossed it off.

No. 2 - A place to live. Pending status.

Within seven days the bank was going to take ownership of my house, and I still had not found us a place to live. In full tilt I headed over to the newspaper rack by the sofa, and filtered through for last week's classifieds. "Maybe I missed something in the home rental section. There's got to be something here."

Bingo! A house for rent for $900.00 a month plus utilities. At present my mortgage payment was a contemptible $500.00 a month, but I was in such exceeding arrears, there was no compromise left with the lender, as I mentioned earlier on. Something spectacular rose up in my spirit, and I just affirmed with myself that this had to be our new home. I made the call and met with the landlords the same day. The house was magnificent and my kids were in awe of it. "Wow, mom!" they whispered. Just seeing the gleam on their faces, I knew I had to make this happen. The owners were an older couple and ironically lived four houses over from their rental property (my new home).

All four of my children were quietly sitting on a long sofa beside me at their home, and so the interview began. They spoke to my children a little and then asked me about myself. After only a few questions they looked at each other to acknowledge they agreed my application was accepted and we could move in right away.

I couldn't believe it! They put a lease together in front of me for one year and I signed it. No credit check of any kind was asked of me. My previous residential address or employment history did not materialize as an issue with my new landlords. I had no idea how I was going to pull this off. I was flat broke and barely into my new job. However, it was a sales job and it was up to me to determine my new destiny.

My children and I lived in that modern 1000 square foot, four bedroom home for ten years. It was a divine appointment that withstood many adversities, and with it sustained many good and fond memories as well.

My children would be more diversified in any opinion of the fond memories. It was a grievous stage for my daughter especially, as I left her alone often to mind the younger ones. This became a serious relationship breaker between us.

– Mad as a hatter –

Getting back to veering into a new life as a single mom, we finally moved in and never looked back. The job was coming along and I was settling in. It was an upscale home for me in an upper scale area that took us from the poverty scale to a middle class status. Although they say appearances can be somewhat misleading, and can involve some smoke and mirrors, either way it was my little miracle!

With the new circumstances revealing a light at the end of the tunnel I became content in my life. The joy of it all lured me back to practicing my singing dream once again. A hook, line and sinker!

There is a fragmentary term called *"bats in the belfry"* which ultimately means someone with an odd behavior. Some might view it as a disjointed or a disconnected demeanor. It's the pre-eminent description of what I became when a sudden shift took place, distracting me from my true responsibilities. In the reflection of that phase I see where I should have refined and brought to balance two passions that seemed to have collided. I was not knowledgeable, wise enough, or with enough applicable judgment to discern where I was headed.

My time was spent on singing and on a handsome man I had just met. Not to mention I was concurrently playing "lawyer" and representing myself in the court room filing motions and affidavits for the divorce proceedings. I was in full swing, settling child visitation and child support issues. I was very busy in my world, and so I indulged selfishly in my own things.

I thought with everything I'd gone through it should be, in theory, my turn to live! It became about me far more than it should have. I will talk more about this later.

29

Have Mercy Judge

I was spending more time in the court room, and preparing documents for my divorce, than I was at my own job. I slept a total of four hours a night at that time. Not being able to afford a lawyer left me with the only option of representing myself, and this for over a year.

A friend of mine who was involved in selling retail franchises across Canada had heard of my familiarities around the court house, and my understanding of filling Court of Queen's Bench motions and affidavits. He was in some sort of bind with his employer, who owed him almost a million dollars in commissions. With my unqualifying resources (being sarcastic) I fundamentally managed to pull together a Statement of Claim together against the company he worked for. I spent a whole night on it at my computer. I finished at 7 in the morning.

As stressful as those times were back and forth in court, I had not realized how therapeutic it was to be on a non-partisan mission. Sink or swim seemed to be the two manageable gears I could shift into, and I was successfully stuck in "swim."

What doesn't feed you makes you stronger. Hunger meets the need to succeed. —**Steve Kaufman**

I walked many times through the Winnipeg Law Courts building, and it was always a unique experience. The ambience and aroma of its well-earned heirship and legacy is breathtaking. Every step taken on its lavishly finished marble floor has an intimidating affluence that fundamentally overtakes you.

I recall one time in particular hearing the loud footsteps of someone behind me, coming out of the same court room where the list of judicial proceedings were to be heard in the chronological order of dockets presented.

The sounds of those steps echoed in the background and they finally caught up to me. There was a tap on my shoulder and a Winnipeg lawyer leaned over and whispered in my ear. "Thought at first you were a lawyer, you handled yourself very well in there, well prepared and a great argument by the way." He concluded with a warm smile and amiably winked at me. I blushed and muttered "Thank you."

It wasn't the first time I had received a compliment for my commitment in doing something I was completely not equipped for but did it anyway. I didn't always succeed, but things were falling into place for me as I was not the kind of person to give up easily on any new obstacle I faced. All of these encumbrances helped me to grow into a problem-solving personality type.

Problems worthy of attack prove their worth by fighting back. —**Piet Hein**

I remember one time running into a woman in a social setting who recognized me. She shared how impressed she was with my determination of not accepting a judge overriding my facts and witnessed my argument as the judge accused me of not providing the courts with the proper paperwork.

I vaguely remember where she worked in the building, but she might have been a stenographer. I had shared with her how I felt the judge was discriminative in the miscalculation of my paperwork. Perhaps the judge felt liberty to do so because I was not an actual lawyer. I was forced to grasp onto a rhetorical jurisdictional world, and none of it was a homespun, simple adjustment for me.

I gave this woman I met a mouthful of inflamed emotions as I felt the judge had erred and I was still sore about it.

I learned quickly all the standard forms required and the protocol of courtroom etiquette. I knew something wasn't right as I had dotted my "I's" and crossed my "T's" on this. I spent many hours in their library researching, and I did comprehend more than they gave me credit for. I was well-prepared.

The conclusions of my court proceedings did end up in The Court of Appeal. This court is the senior and final court in the province of Manitoba. Getting this right for me was crucial. Just when I thought I was over my head in my appeal application, I received a call from the Court of Appeal office and the clerk encouraged me by providing me with a sample of a Factum and Book of Appeal by one of Winnipeg's prominent lawyers, Hersh Wolch. It was fantastic. I followed the same guidelines like it was a puzzle, carefully placing all the pieces for a perfect fit. Thanks to the clerk's assistance I had it all done in less than seven days.

Putting together a Factum and a Book of Appeal for the Court of Appeal is by no definition an easy task, even for a seasoned lawyer. It's a lot of work. The court provides a window of many weeks to complete the application process for the final submission, which is reviewed first prior to accepting. Like a table of contents check list, everything must be in order.

– A premium seat –

The Court of Appeal is generally comprised of three judges, who constitute a quorum. But once in a while it will be a panel of five judges on matters of greater importance.

If I could enlighten this further, it was sort of an amusing process. On the day of my Court of Appeal I was the only one unaccounted for in the dress code, which required that judges and lawyers wear a black and white robe. I was a stumblingly misfit at my podium, representing myself without the bona-fide formal attire. Without a law degree I did not earn the privilege of this apparel. There were three judges in black and white robes who were sitting on a bench so high I swear my neck was locked in that "looking up" position for the rest of the day.

I believe the formal word for a raised platform is a "dais." It is primarily considered a throne or a seat of honor to allow the judges to view the entire courtroom. The bench is raised above the surrounding level to distinguish prominence. To the average lay person this is an extremely intimidating setting. It's an atmosphere of reverence, respect, adoration, and even worship. It can be a trembling experience if you don't understand the sophistication of the etiquette and court rulings it fosters.

Until you have set foot in a Court of Appeal or the Supreme Court, which is the highest Court, you have not experienced what it is like to be before a king. It is grand, deserving, and warrants your pledge to honor the moment you step foot in its royal residence. —SM

On the inside I was panic-stricken and scared to death. On the outside I assumed the role of a lawyer and played the game. My husband's lawyer's factum was horrific and was primarily based on assumptions, whereas mine was based on facts. It became an easier argument at my end. For the purposes of this book let's call my husband's lawyer "Joan." She continued to talk over me and interrupt me. She assumed (like her factum) The Court of Appeal Judges would see favor with her as I was not a lawyer and she was. However, there was a quick shift when one of the three judges asked her to stop talking. "We will let you know when it's your turn to speak."

I now had the floor, and all the judges, except for one, seemed to be attentive to my words. I will never forget this judge, the one to my left. He was busy with the eye rolling, shrugging and nodding while I was in the middle of my explanation about why I did not need an affidavit for a past motion I did in the Court of Queen's Bench. This in part was what had forced me to apply for an appeal. I needed to continue this motion from the Court of Queen's Bench, where a judge basically threw me out of her court for not filing properly. Inevitably it turned out that my paper work was correct.

The judge to my left continued to look around the room as though I were not speaking. "You find this amusing, do you?" My words projected across the room in an emphatic echo, right into his ears. "Excuse me?" as he cautiously removed his glasses in a stunned yet disgusted manner.

"Do you have any; I mean any idea what court you are in?" he asked. "Yes," I eloquently responded to him, as I affirmed that I was in the highest trial court in Manitoba.

There was silence between us, and awkwardly he was trying to figure out what to say to me next. Meanwhile the other two judges seem to be holding back a modest smirk. "Well then," he says, with one bushy eyebrow leaning in, "tell me why you think that I would think this is amusing." He pushed his glasses down to the tip of his nose. Easy question, I thought, somewhat relieved that I was not going to jail for contempt. I cannot recall my words verbatim, but in my voicing to the judge I remember expressing the following: "As a judge," I said, "you should be reinforcing my confidence and looking at me directly when I speak. I am here with only one opportunity to be before you and this should be respected. Your demeanor tells me that you have bias against me before my argument or explanation has even concluded." I reiterated that I expected him to hold his posture, and to focus on me when it was my turn to talk. I was very categorical about him not rolling his eyes when I was speaking.

Although my experience with that one judge might be interpreted as scolding, this was not the case. For me it was about holding my own, and standing up for myself when I thought I was being treated unfairly. I had nothing to lose, with my one chance to assert myself and without a care as to what anyone thought. It was quite liberating!

———————

You can't lead me down that road. —**Taylor Swift**

———————

30

Nest Egg

The appeal court was almost at a close. The judge on the left was extremely on the ball now, and he had his eye on the sparrow. In a few regaling moments, though, I would test him while conversing with one of the other two judges and quickly glancing over to see where he was looking. Seemingly he focused well on my words when I spoke and he had a new acquiescent and polished posture. It was worth my vindication.

In conclusion of the long and short of my Court of Appeal ruling, I won! Sort of… then I lost….sort of…!

I won in part, primarily because of the middle judge. He conceded that my findings on a previous established case that had set precedents did warrant that I was correct; and therefore concluded that the judge from the Court of Queen's Bench had erred.

The middle judge seemed to be the one in control of that courtroom, and so it was him I knuckled down on. The other two judges just seemed to follow his lead and so I selected him to prevail upon.

Just when I thought I had won him over on the first part of my appeal, he (they) imputed and opposed the second request, which was in relation to a "Motion to Stay" I had previously filed for the Court of Queen's Bench.

Now that it was all over, "Joan" (my husband's lawyer) got her opportunity and jumped up to her podium, demanding that I pay court costs in her dictatorial "pay the piper" attitude!

The middle judge stepped up to the plate to deal with Joan's request head on. He didn't acknowledge her but rather leaned forward, and with great empathy he looked me square in the eyes and said, "Give me one good reason why you, Suzanne Mariani, should not pay court cost." Wow! I didn't see that coming, and I thought to myself "this is one smart, accomplished, discerning, and understanding Judge." He was providently far-sighted with an affluence of wisdom through the entire process. How could anyone not honor this type of poise and nobility? He was giving me an "out" and all I had to do was sell him on it. And so I did! Case closed!

In the previous chapter I shared with you about my friend who had an employer who owed him approximately one million dollars in commissions. At least that's what he told me. I put together a Statement of Claim for him, which I worked on all night, and then had him sign the next day. I had not done this before, buy "Hey, it's just a document," I thought. "I'll fill in the blanks."

Ideas are easy. It's the execution of ideas that really separates the sheep from the goats. —**Sue Grafton**

Well, it was fantastically creative! It was one of those pat myself on the back moments with a little dance in my step singing "Good Job - Good Job - Good Job!"

It can get confusing. I truly wanted to help my friend and I was at the same time finding myself working through balancing accomplishments without shouting them out to the streets. "Look what I did!"

Rick Warren, a noted author, states: "Humility is not thinking less of yourself; it is thinking of yourself less. Humility is thinking more of others."

Needing recognition is a sign of dysfunction and insecurity. A problem I've struggled with most of my life due to the transgressor called "unworthiness."

Thank goodness for the friends who stuck by me in all those times without tossing me overboard, even when I deserved it. They stuck by me, corrected me, chastised me and loved me all at the same time.

Although it was a balancing act of emotions, I tried to stay focused as much as I could.

Impatience, rage, and insecurities were still brewing in me from my past, as I was not yet refined in the school of healing myself, nor was I balanced in my character.

It was a work in progress, and these types of projects, like my friend who needed help, were virile to me. They helped me stay in a sound and healthy mind with a mission that was like an arrow going one way. And I needed to hit my target. I had lost my will too many times in my life and so I grabbed whatever fed me "life" again.

Projects! Projects! Projects!

I sent my friend with the completed Statement of Claim to the Law Courts building to have it stamped and filed against his employer, the franchisor. I then asked him to make as many copies as he had sold franchises to, and then send via fax each franchisee a copy of the claim.

The Statement of Claim indicated that the franchisor, who had the rights to the franchise name, had not given each franchisee owner a kickback, which was an entitlement any time a franchise store was sold.

"This," I told my friend, "will probably cause each franchise owner to demand the kickbacks they should have received, and the end result may be a class action suit against your employer. You're the whistle-blower on this and they will love you for it! You'll undeniably be their sweet huckleberry!"

Onward to putting an ad in the newspaper, I sent the story via fax to the editor's desk but didn't sign my name to it. I made my friend, who wanted his million, the main contact, and the story was published a few days later.

The phone never stopped ringing, and every franchisee in Canada who received and read the Statement of Claim had dialed my friend's number within the hour. It was like the outhouse had collided with the windmill. Splash!

In the myriad of all these phone calls the franchisor's lawyer contacted my friend to meet with him at his office along with his employer, who had rights to the franchise name.

"It's pay day!" he thought. And it was! He never told me what they settled on, but he was one happy camper.

I assumed there was a gag order and they took his phone away to keep him from having contact with any of the franchisees who were "hot on the trail" to get their kickbacks. When I asked why he was calling me from a pay phone he said "They have my phone, end of story!"

If I was a lawyer I suppose I could say I won, sort of… !!

But since I was not licensed to practice law, I did not expect to get paid for the services rendered. However, he was kind enough to look after a few of my outstanding household bills that had piled up over time. He was very grateful that I had orchestrated this brilliantly, he said.

Today my friend is busy, investing and selling commercial properties in many countries.

He makes certain he gets paid straight up with no holdbacks from anyone anymore.

———————————

Your best teacher is your last mistake. —**Ralph Nader**

———————————

————————➤●⊂————————

31

Game Plan

One more project completed! I was driven for some reason to take on things I'd never taken on before. Oddly enough, I was fascinated with the flashing ideas that scurried through my mind like a mouse running across the room. Then, boom, they were gone out of my head if I didn't process them quickly enough. Looking back, many people considered me as an opinionated personality, but for me it was an expression of ideas I had to quickly get out or I'd forget. I am not alone in this struggle with Attention Deficit Hyperactivity Disorder (ADHD).

Although, I have never been diagnosed fully, it was a reality in my life, and I believe it was developed through my own anxieties over time. These insecurities were in connection to the tumultuous war zone in my thinking, having felt neglected and depressed most of my life.

Being pessimistic and distrustful while feeling dejected is a key that locks you into a destructive mental state and temperament. —SM

Still working on my insecurities, I was aware of my thought patterns and found myself still slipping in and out of past behaviors. When would I get rid of the old me and become the new me? This was hard to do without mentors but I read many self-help books as mentioned earlier on, and I knew I had gotten this far "so I just have to keep going," I would tell myself over and over.

Forgiving yourself, when others don't want to, is equally a crushing challenge. For me, I had affirmed that a seal was on my heart with a scripted truth that I was on the road to recover, to heal, to learn and to grow.

With all the good intentions I had, it was extremely hard on my four children while I was raising them and simultaneously working on the path of trying to fix me at the same time. Such a simple answer would have been what Jesus of Nazareth taught – *Count others more significant than yourselves. Let each of you look not only to his own interests, but also to the interests of others. Philippians 2:4*

Focusing on others takes your mind off you. That was great for a few days, and then I'd slip up again. *Proverbs 7:23 is a powerful statement that rings true – "So what a man thinks so shall he be."*

Here's the problem I believe most of us face: we get sidetracked and distracted easily on any new resolution or positive change that we sincerely want to make for ourselves. Doing the right thing is often harder than doing the wrong thing. We are so conditioned to our familiar behaviors that "change" doesn't come easy, and it can't be done successfully without the unerring volition of discipline.

Something that can't happen until we aim for it first!

Building something solid like an apartment block in many ways is similar to building and grooming yourself for personal growth. Although one is considered to be a tangible build and the other intangible, they both include some form of nuts and bolts to hold them together. It doesn't just appear. It begins with the idea first, then to paper, to tools, then to the ground up. Dedicated exertions of labor will ultimately promise to create what you've envisioned, as a final refinement of perfection.

A new building is fresh and strong when finished. But if the winds and the storms of this world hit hard enough and we don't have the proper provisions for the maintenance, then the walls will begin to crumble quickly.

That's where many of us get stuck. It can be too late to rebuild so a demolition is our only option. Like the potter who finds something wrong with the pot of clay and reshapes it all over again to mold it to the piece it was meant to be.

It is a very important part of growing when we understand it's ok to be reshaped and remolded. It's ok to be brought down to be brought up. It's ok to take two steps back for three forward. It's ok to make the mistakes that are designed to bring about change in your life. (Even if you have to do it over and over.)

Like the potter's clay I became ready to be shaped, but it was a long time at the wheel for the potter to change this vessel. It's been a long road for change.

I have learned that trouble is the wound of greatness and can be used for our good. You cannot acquire a fine flowered perfume without crushing the flower first.

To improve is to change; to be perfect is to change often. —**Winston Churchill**

Since my established change was not easy, in the hindsight of things, I wish the chronic ache in my heart of how it affected my children would have gripped me much sooner.

My "It's my turn to live" attitude was an expensive mistake that cost me greatly. Neglecting the needs of my then teenage daughter came with a set-back of losing many quality years with her. An extravagant error on my part. I was inordinately sluggish in the understanding of how much she needed me, and inevitably I failed her many times. And this with much regret.

I was too busy finding myself, like an old cliché. To receive forgiveness from my children is more important to me today than any dream I've ever followed. Fortunately these mistakes are behind me, and every day is a new day that is fresh with every new conversation or time I have with them.

Getting back to those years when the kids were teenagers, singing was back on my "things to do list" during any spare time I had. I also became quite compulsive about jogging daily, sometimes up to three half marathons a week. Crazy but true!

At that time I was on the go and socializing with people in the business spectrum. I was enchanted by the impetus energy of power it brought into my life. Being in sales seemed to grant access to meeting many eligible single men. It was to me somewhat refreshing to enjoy so many male companionships. I was mostly attracted to businessmen, or maybe they were attracted to me.

With all the networking I was now involved in, I was unexpectedly struck with two marriage proposals. They were financially wealthy men and I was ambivalent to both.

Like hitting gold, I had dates coming out of my ears. Since I was busy and in the mode of pushing for myself a music career, I was too short-sighted to see that some of these men were starting to fall in love with me.

One of them promised I would never have to work another day in my life. "Let's go for it," he said. The other perceived that I was the only woman for him, and said he couldn't stop thinking about me.

Wow, but no thanks. *I'm out!*

32

Hobnob

Although I did not have a step by step system, I was moving forward. I was renting a beautiful home with a spacious yard overlooking greenery and a beautiful marsh with deer often running through my back yard. I had a modest sales job and I was focused on a possible music career.

I wasn't where I used to be, and this was my confident assurance to a straight path of freedom.

I was introduced to a Winnipeg producer who was an incredible musician/singer/songwriter. Chris Burke-Gaffney was a pillar in the industry, and ran an A1 class recording studio. He started his career as a singer/bassist for The Pumps (Polygram). He signed his first record deal as a teenager and toured with acts like Triumph, Guns N' Roses, and AC/DC. In his early twenties, he wrote his first top-ten single, "Miracle," for Orphan. His early songs continue to receive heavy airplay on classic rock radio.

When I met with Chris he was very supportive. I had shared with him the prodigious opposition I had from friends and some family members, who didn't agree with my aspirations to sing.

We spent many long hours in his studio, sometimes just talking about life. He gave me many reassuring reasons to keep moving ahead as a singer in spite of anyone's opinion. "It's your dream," he would say.

I didn't have much money, so we compromised by making an album without using live instruments. Seeing that I was short on songs to complete the album, Chris graciously offered several songs he had co-written. Walking in the studio one day he said "'Hey there sista, I've written a song for you called "I'll Be Here" and it'll be perfect for your album." He was right.

Chris Burke-Gaffney was not someone who minced his words; he was a straight shooter on his points and never needed to rationalize or show cause. The studio was his baby and he knew his way around it. Once he sat in that production chair it was magic from there.

For me, the song "I'll Be Here" mirrors the spiritual side of things. It breathes a reassurance that we are never alone. Chris and I had engaged on the topic of God one time, and I shared with him how that was an important segment of my life. Keeping that in mind he wrote the song to reflect just that.

I don't remember where I had lunch last week, and yet there are things that people can say or do for me that are scripted in my heart for a lifetime. For me this is one of them. The song today would probably be noted as outdated by some standards, but the production was fabulous. It was and is a song I've listened to over and over again in my car. Especially when I need to deposit a truth that we are never really alone; there will always be someone that will love and support us even in times of deep opposition. "I'll Be Here" says it all!

– Gold star friends –

With an unwavering driving force for my singing passion, an acquaintance of mine was prompted to make a call, and then briskly handed me the phone. I heard this sweet and gentle voice at the other end. "Hello Suzanne, how are you? And nice to finally meet you even if it's over the phone," she continued. "Brian has told me all about you and the fire you have for the music industry."

"I'm sorry, you are who"? I asked.

"My name is Stoney Figueroa."

"Am I supposed to know you?" I asked.

"Aawh"... no worries," she responded, "let me fill you in a little. I was one of the Ikettes."

"The who?" I asked.

"Not The Who," she awkwardly chuckled, "The Ikettes." I felt an air of smugness as she cleared her throat. "I was part of a trio of female backing vocalists and dancers for Ike and Tina Turner. I've been an entertainer for many years. Brian thought it would be a good idea to connect with you and told me if he met up with you he would make sure to hook us up, and here we are!"

"Yes, ma'am, here we are!" I said.

It was a compelling conversation and since that phone call I met with Stonye in California many times. She eventually moved to Vegas, but that didn't stop the ongoing and meaningful friendship we still hold dear today. She calls me her white BFF, all in fun of course. Stonye is no ordinary entertainer; she is vivacious with the energy that stretches like an elastic band. Barely 5'4" weighing in at about 100 lbs, nothing holds her down.

She rocks the stage with energy like I've never seen. Similarly many of us who dream big can sometimes end up in the shadows of someone else's success. Not everyone who tries will be the star of the show. It is not easy for any entertainer, or anyone who labors many exhausting hours, months and years, to come to the place of true success.

And all aiming for that one spot on stage.

Stonye was a trooper and kept her pace. She never saw herself as unfortunate because she was only a backup singer/dancer for Ike and Tina Turner. A victim she was not. She rather embellished in all her successes and embraced the idea of knowing she was still living out the great opportunity she had as an artist. Over a thousand women wanted to audition to be one of the Ikettes, and when Stonye was up it was hands down, her new gig with Ike and Tina Turner.

Stonye and Bobby Kato Drake, her now ex, took considerable good care of me when I travelled to California. They were quite the pair, and total opposites of one another. There were no inhibitions between them, as they would say what was on their mind in front of me as though I was not present. This was awkward and uncomfortable at the beginning but ironically enough I realized it was because they felt safe with me, like being part of the family.

Bobby, no stranger to the entertainment industry himself, was a body guard on special touring events for singers like Michael Jackson, Aretha Franklin and Rick James. He was the personal body guard for one of the world's most famous R&B performers, which today is still considered as The Motown Super Group, "The Temptations!"

Bobby was the social guy who loved to network in the industry he loved. We all know someone like that, the "go to" guy! He talked to everyone and seemed to know everyone, some on the front lines and others on the sidelines. Hanging out with Stonye and Bobby was an adventure every night I was out in Los Angeles. For fun Bobby would say "Name an event that's in Hollywood and I'll see if I can get us in tonight." Most of the time it wasn't too challenging for him and he'd proudly make it happen. With every visit, I was always made to feel like a special guest. It was like paying for an elite tour guide but better.

Our relationship allowed me to meet many interesting people. On the night of the 2007 Grammys, there was a world peace song recording that was taking place with many elite singers involved. Stonye was scheduled for it. Guess who got to piggy back on that one? Yes, I was included in the group singing and it was fantastic to be part of this recording. Unfortunately the song was never released.

The recording producer for the world peace song was John Wilson, who was known for his varying and diverse talents. You will find out more about John further on.

I had visited Hollywood several times but the busiest I've ever been was the week of the Grammys in 2007. Stonye had me on my toes with things to do and sights to see. I considered it a colossal holiday.

Stonye Figueroa and Bobby Kato Drake

33

Miss The Boat

Like clockwork, I would get a panic and /or anxiety attack within hours of arriving in Los Angeles. Pulling over on the busiest highways to calm myself down was not an unusual ritual for me. The air was different and it would trigger an old anxiety that made me feel like I was in a serious panic attack. I would put on the blinkers in my rental car, breathe deep and remind myself with a little self-talk that I was ok and that panic was no longer a part of my life. Usually after a fifteen minute meditation time I was back to a normal balanced and calm life until the next one would hit. They were getting further and further apart, so life was getting richer.

Smile, breathe and go slowly. —**Thich Nhat Hanh**

Stonye called. "Get here for noon," she said. "We are going for lunch today with Chris Mancini." "Who?" I asked in my ignorance. "Chris Mancini," she repeated. "He is the son of the renowned and famous Henry Mancini." She continued to tell me an impressive history of this man's father.

"He won twenty Grammy Awards, a Golden Globe, four Academy Awards, and a posthumous Grammy Lifetime Achievement Award. Maybe you will remember the Pink Panther theme," she said.

"Hello, are you still there?" I was so dazzled by her explanation I was dumbfounded. "Yup, I get it now," I said, trying to play the "I'm cool as a cucumber" role. "His son Chris," she went on to say, "is also exceptionally talented. He is noted for his EDM music productions in Los Angeles. He and I have been talking about doing some work together, and I want you to meet him."

It was a fantastic lunch and one that is memorable to me. Chris and I spoke again another time but I was not in a financial position to continue as the costs of working with him would be higher than I could possibly afford, and I still had kids at home. It was one of my regrets with such a great opportunity in front of me. However, even in hindsight it would have been dangerous to choose that over my children's needs, bills and groceries for my family. I accepted my loss of that opportunity but somehow kept the dream alive.

On the evening of the Grammys, after the recording for The Peace Song, Stonye and Bobby were heading out to the after party. "You're coming with us," Stonye shouted from across the room. "Really!?" I was so excited.

So off we went in my rental car. Something I insisted on every time I traveled there and spent time with them. They could expect me to be their chauffeur and to cover all gas expenses. I didn't drink alcohol so it was a collaborated delight that I also became the designated driver. It was a fair reciprocation as they were perfect hosts on all my visits.

Making our way to the Grammy after party, I had no idea where we were headed on the road other than the directions being given to me by Bobby. Coming to a stop at our destination I couldn't help but notice the countless luxury vehicles in front of us. We were all lined up patiently to enter into a large commercial or studio type property. One car at a time, a security person peeped through each driver's side and asked for identification. With a clipboard in hand, a search was made to match each name on the list. Once the pen scripted a check mark you were in. "Please drive through and enjoy your evening" was repeatedly heard with each car passing through the check point for invited guests only.

Once inside, the venue layout was defined to complement a warm and casual setting. Round pub tables were spread out for moderate mingling among the guests. There was only one empty table left, and so I promptly seated myself. While Stonye and Bobby were busy across the room blending in with a group of people they recognized, I spotted the actor Patrick Swayze. He was sitting at the table next to me, which was so close I could literally reach over to shake his hand. *Should I say hello?* I was thinking. *Maybe I should tell him how much I enjoyed watching him in the movie Dirty Dancing or Ghost.*

Rehearsing all the options of what to say to him resulted in my having exhausted thoughts. I was so dumbfounded in my loss for words that I ended up saying nothing.

I'm at a loss for words. But even my loss is amplified.
—Talib Kweli

I decided to leave the table to meet up with Stonye and Bobby, who were stock-stilled in the same location, busy with their schmoozing, especially Bobby.

As I pulled the chair away Patrick Swayze looked directly at me and sent a warm smile. Still clammed up in a closed-mouth, I settled to just reciprocate a smile in return, with no words spoken.

Patrick Swayze died two years later of pancreatic cancer, and I have considerable regret about not telling him when the opportunity presented itself how much I enjoyed his movies.

He was loved as an actor with many successful movies that will inevitably grant him honor for many years to come.

The evening came to a close "What a jammed packed week," I sighed on the way back to my hotel, just before dropping off Bobby and Stonye. We began to chat further about the meeting that Stonye set up for me to meet Ike Turner. I can't remember if it was the afternoon of or the day before the 2007 Grammy night.

Our time was short with Ike, yet I was grateful even for a summarized time slot. Straight to the point, he complimented me on my vocals, mentioning he had listened to the songs I sent when we exchanged emails months prior. Having worked so hard at learning to sing, his words were an enchanting ballot.

Because he was up for a Grammy, he expounded a few times about it during our meeting. Being a blues singer at the time, I was very intrigued. He seemed restless and critical on a few matters, and shared his grumble about not enjoying the drive to the hotel. He mentioned a few times that his feet were sore. (Funny how one can remember these details.)

Yet there I was standing in front of a renowned rock'n roll pioneer, an R&B veteran, and a nominee for the music industry's highest honor, a Grammy! His son, Ike Junior, was with him and they spoke more of themselves as a team.

On a note of history, Ike and Tina Turner were inducted into the Rock and Roll Hall of Fame in 1991. He was now 75 years old, and took home the traditional blues album award for "Risin."

I became fascinated with the music industry as it was a new discovery for me since I had taught myself to sing. Learning from seasoned musicians and singers was a riveting confidence booster to say the least.

34

Midas Touch

With finances still in a crunch, I often found it staggering how I was able to travel and to continue recording in studios with all the towering high costs that came with it.

I wanted to press forward in my life, and my idea of "I can do anything" was now real on the inside.

Like anything else that takes time to build, so does believing in oneself. —SM

I remember one day during work hours pausing at my desk for a brief moment. I went into a compendious thinking mode that presumably made me to appear to be in some sort of daydreaming zone. While glaring over at an empty wall, within my heart I was having a conversation. First with me, then with God!

I could feel the sigh in my heart, and the heaviness of never breaking free from the job I was in. It was fine for the phase in my life when I was first hired but with times changing so had my needs. The future now seemed limited and the commission structure was not geared to be prosperous enough to keep up with the ongoing growth of my family or my dreams.

Although I was sitting at my desk quietly, in my heart I was kneeling. There was a bending going on inside of me that was sincere and, come what may, it was for me an unfailing virtuous humility. With this private inward moment I began to pray a simple prayer:

"Dear God, I need you right now. My struggles of being stuck and not being able to move forward are hard for me to bear. I am discouraged and need sound guidance. I feel I'm in a semblance of being cemented to these walls of my work and there seems to be no breaking. Reveal yourself to me so that I know you have heard me, and bring to me an opportunity so I can break free from these chains of not being able to make ends meet. Amen."

As I pulled away from my desk I happened to notice out of the corner of my eye a newspaper that was left on a filing cabinet close by. I noticed the papers were shambled, slumped over and ready to slide down. I hurried to catch the first page before it plummeted to the floor, and noticed it was the classified job section.

I immediately got curious and reviewed all the sales ads, and there it was. My dream job!

A high profile homebuilder was looking for a salesperson to sell their new homes, and they were offering a pretty hefty commission. I never would have believed this infallible truth had I not lived it out myself. The process was perfect, and nothing could stop the inevitable that it took only one motivation, one prayer, one ad, one phone call, one interview, and let's simply wrap it up, I got hired. End of story!

Not only did they hire me, even though I had no idea how to do this job, they agreed to give me a three month salary to ensure financial security prior to the launch of a straight commission pay. This was opportunity!

It wasn't until late that evening a remembrance of that prayer was thought of and duly noted upon my thankful heart.

The interview was mind-blowing. One of the owners presented their business mission statement, the type of homes they built, how they built, the demographics of age groups they primarily served and the quality of their final and noble product. "Our customers," he said, "are generally lawyers, doctors, and business owners. A million dollar home isn't for everyone," he said.

They were an established elite home builder then, and even today their reputation of excellence continues.

Expensive but Luxurious!

It was approximately a half hour of the owner speaking and half an hour of me listening; an unusual task for me, as I love to chat. I generally like to begin, not end. However, there was a cue that pointed me in a direction to stay focused on what I believed I could do well.

I knew how to sell and close on a deal. I didn't give him a chance to discuss homebuilding anymore as I was fixed on my pursuing him to hire me because I knew once I knew my product inside and out, I could take it from there. I told him I would complete any transaction I began, and help every client get from point A to point B. A promise I never failed this company to keep.

Both brothers agreed that I was a shoe-in for the job. Seven years later, with few holidays, I dedicated myself to selling their homes with little time off, working seven days a week. I was the face they trusted with their brand, and they were not ashamed to put me in the front lines.

With hard work, long hours, and the sales of many homes, I was finally able to put money away to purchase a home for myself. In two years, I had saved up a security deposit of $30,000.00. It was something I could never have done on my own without a life-changing decision.

Since homebuilding was becoming such a growing industry, the company decided to hire another salesperson. This for me caused a feeling of being disjointed at my job as I did not know how to split our territories, customers, hours at the show home etc. I was the girl who did everything and involved myself in every aspect of each project we built. How was sharing my business going to work?

I did everything in my power to follow through in my job and with all my customers. The new person they hired seemed to want to top me in everything. If I said blue she would say "wrong color." Even when I agreed on a solution to a work-related problem she would find another conflict and face me head on with it. She was an extremely confrontational person, bold and direct.

Although I had more experience than her with this company, she was radically convincing to the owners that everything I did was unsubstantial, in error, and off-target. We were a successful business and yet somehow she lured them into believing I never knew what I was talking about and they should have hired her long ago.

Being confident with the business current high volume sales, they decided at a sales meeting to run with most of her ideas in spite of my objections and reasoning. She was a fresh new face to them and they were going to run with it.

You can fool all of the people some of the time, and some of the people all of the time, but you cannot fool all of the people all of the time. **—Abraham Lincoln**

As she continued to belabor her point of my conduct, and the systems I put in place that annoyed her, I decided to have a cool head about it and accepted the conflict without a squabble.

While she was poisoning the office with her tall tales, I was busy dreaming how to break out of there for a new chapter.

— Music makes the medicine go down—

I decided that a getaway might help. I took a short vacation from the office and headed to California. Stonye and Bobby were once again busy setting me up to attend some really cool events. This trip, however, was a combination of not only pleasure but of business. I met with John Wilson who in a previous chapter I shared was the producer for the Peace Song at the 2007 Grammy night, which I participated in. I have an immense respect for John and his knowledge of the industry. There isn't a question he can't answer when it comes to producing, writing, or copyright. He's masterfully skilled in understanding the letter of the law in the music industry, which is sophistically intricate and legally entangling.

John is always in full swagger when it comes to his own self-portrayal of music. (Savoir-faire)   He's done it all.

He's a co-founding member of the original Sly Slick & Wicked rhythm and blues band. They have been inducted into the R&B Hall of Fame and displayed in the Rock & Roll Hall of Fame in Cleveland Ohio.

"I've got these songs," he said, before I left Winnipeg for California. "My buddies wrote the music and maybe if I pass along to you, you can put lyrics and melodies to them and we can record them when you arrive in California."

"Awesome," I said. "Who are your buddies?" "Ralf Johnson," he said, "a member of the band Earth, Wind and Fire, and Amir Bayyan of Kool and the Gang." Without any room to breathe, I began to sing one of the Kool and the Gang's hit song "Celebrate good times c'mon." A sweet chuckle came out of John on the phone and he responded, "Yes, that was one of their greatest hits!" With scads of excitement I said, "Send the songs over, John. I'm in!"

Unfortunately I didn't have enough time to finish putting melodies and lyrics to the songs John sent me as my flight had already been booked and scheduled to leave within a few days.

With quick timing I managed to make arrangements and wrap up all the details for the kids to be looked after while I was away. With all the stress of what I was going through at work, I was feeling very empowered to finally have some alone time, visit with my friends, enjoy some recording time, and lastly to focus on something other than my job.

With a good night sleep, I was bright-eyed, bushy-tailed and ready for my five day adventure in California.

The flight was very uncomfortable for many of the passengers, with the aggravating nuisance of turbulence. For me it was a muffled background and not a distraction.

Up until the point of landing I was busy writing lyrics, and humming melodies and harmonies under my breath, to complete the songs and have them ready for John.

We were recording that afternoon and I didn't want to tell him I couldn't finish.

Writers often tortue themselves trying to get the words right. Sometimes you must lower your expectations and just finish it. —**Don Roff**

35

In The Hock

Once in the studio with John I met Lu, another producer. He had a pit bull that seemed to be uneasy and suspicious of me. With his legs apart and chest thrown out he stared directly into my eyes. Convinced that he would attack, I lost my composure immediately, and yielded to fear. Frozen in one spot, unable to move, I asked Lu to remove the dog. After a few laughs amongst themselves, in their confidence that the dog would not hurt a fly, they continued to work around me while I was paralyzed with fear.

After a few minutes had gone by, I still hadn't budged from my spot. Lu leaned over to me and said, "You really are afraid of this dog, aren't you?" "Yes," I said. "I won't be able to record with your dog here." "No problem," he responded, "I will take care of it and put the dog in another room. I apologize for this. Not everyone is afraid of him; he's like the mascot of the studio."

Once the dog was gone I was in full swing to be myself, and comfortable enough to sing with ease. We completed three songs within a few days, and that gave me more time to hang out with Stonye and Bobby. Of course Bobby had done his usual networking. He got us into all sorts of exciting events in Hollywood that happened to be Invitation only. "I may be married to him," Stonye would say, "but I still have no idea how he pulls it off."

It was time to come back and face the music at work. When I returned to the office nothing seemed normal. The way we were meeting with clients was now changing, they had revamped the system I had put in place for clients, and the new girl got the territory she wanted. Our sales meetings became shaky and without harmony. She shot down every idea until I got up from a meeting one day and said, "Why don't I let you all figure this out without me, and let me know later what you've decided."

Exhausted and tired, I surrendered and complied with almost everything they wanted. I was in the same place I was with my last job. It was a phase of perfect timing in the beginning with all of its increase, but this season too was coming to an end. (la fins)

Problems at home escalated as well, as one of my twins decided to run away. I called the police, but they wanted twenty-four hours notice to place a missing persons report. Between all of us in the family searching, we finally figured out where he might be. He had met a girl who was involved with drugs and alcohol, and she somehow mesmerized him with her charm. He was trying to fill the hole in his life, the one that I should have filled by being there for him when he needed me. He was going down the tubes and I was just dying inside to find him, to love him, and to help him.

When we found him, it felt like it was too late to protect and love him. He had issues and felt trapped, with much deserved anger towards me. I needed to win his love and trust again. I considered that an earned privilege, and I was willing to do whatever was necessary. I wasn't home very much, and I knew this was the catalyst for change.

Your children need your presence more than your presents. —Jesse Jackson

---

We spent hours talking, and I gave him a lot more attention than I had in the past. One day there was a knock on the door, and it was that girl. It was like he had an addiction to her and to her lifestyle of drugs and alcohol, yet with her it was an addiction to him, to keep him in her spiraling web. My son had come to realize the destruction of this dependency and was choosing the breaking point as an occasion to be set free from her entanglement.

Opening the door, I said "The relationship is over and there is no reason for you to come here." I was displaying a little bravery, hoping my son was not close by and able to hear this. I continued, "He's tried over and over to tell you to leave him alone, but you just don't give up."

Benjamin Mee, motivational speaker and author of "We Bought a Zoo", once said, "Sometimes all you need is 20 seconds of insane courage. Just, literally, 20 seconds of just embarrassing bravery. And I promise you, something great will come of it."

I advised her to get some help, but she was not accepting of it and was slurring words in her inebriated state. Her language became foul, and I ultimately had no choice but to close the door on her.

Across the street I watched as she sat on the curb, drunk and unglued. She was hoping to catch my son walk out, but he was comfortable at home watching television. I said a prayer for her (under my breath) as it was heartbreaking for me to see her lost and off balance at such a young age.

When I thought about going back out to talk to her, she was already gone.

Although my son was not impressed that I took it upon myself to speak for him, in the end he was content with it. A grace I've always appreciated.

The next day I was back in the office, hoping I could clear my head enough to concentrate on the other problems I was facing. I prepared my paperwork for my early appointment. I had clients meeting me in the hopes of building their dream home. I laid out the plans I thought they might be interested in. When the receptionist buzzed me to announce they had arrived, I had forgotten they had a real estate agent that would be joining us.

As we all sat together in our discussions about buying land, choosing the type of home to build, and creating a budget, all I could think about was "Why don't I become a realtor®?"

I couldn't wait to make a phone call to the Real Estate Board and enquire. I was well versed in land development and I had a good understanding of plans, working daily with drafts people on all our client custom design homes. I was not part of the construction team, and yet very involved in all the home building stages, and I knew most of the trades on hand. With every new build I monitored the status in terms of construction and finishing stages. My experience was a firm confidence that I truly was a point "A" to "Z" new home specialist for all of my clients.

On the same day I enquired about costs of getting my real estate license, the other girl they hired to co-operate in home sales had once again pulled a fast one. She had gone directly to the owners and claimed one of my clients was actually hers. Without speaking to me the file was transferred, and it became her new account.

This was my breaking point to do something and to do it quick. I decided to get my Real Estate License, and I carried on through my job with or without the troubles in the office, as I knew I had a new chapter to move forward to.

It wasn't easy studying and learning from these books that had cost me a small fortune. Math is not my strong point, and is considered to be my least favorite four letter word.

The Winnipeg Real Estate course is no fast ticket for a real estate license, if you're not fresh out of school. There are three phases which each offer a six month time frame to complete, and three hours of exams for each one. (Looking back that was twelve hours of exams for me instead of nine; I had failed the first and had to re-do it.)

The day came, and at last I held in my hand a Winnipeg Real Estate license. This was for me the end of the old and the beginning of the new.

If I could break down the meaning in a mix of Italian and French, it would be an import of "finito" to the job, "la fins" to the new girl who marred my job, and "nouveaux" to a fresh new start.

Important note: Several years went by, and I ran into the agent who pushed me out of my job with the builder I had otherwise been well established in. She apologized to me with much remorse in her heart. There were many situational struggles and issues at the time, and she was not herself. "I had so much anger in me about other things going on in my life that I was reacting to everything in trying to find my own space," she said. "And this I did with a hard heart," she continued, "I'm so sorry!" That was a healing moment for us both. And so I forgave, hugged and thanked her for those mending words. We were both able to move forward.

———◦———

36

Score

My first year in real estate was challenging, as I was used to having clients come to me, and now I was chasing after clients. With the homebuilder it was easier to find people as I did not pay for any advertising; they did it all.

Every morning I asked myself the same questions: "Where do I find someone who wants to buy a house? And where do I find someone who wants to list their house?" While everyone was busy online and using their savvy internet skills, I did what was simple and traditional. Something I could understand and relate to. Seven years with the homebuilder taught me something about myself. I was darn good at hosting an open house.

Every person walking through the door is a prospect.

This is Rule #1.

Rule #2 - Never ignore anyone coming through your open house, no matter how busy you are.

Rule #3 - Take everyone's name and phone number. (Ask why they stopped in.)

Rule #4 - If you notice something positive about them, boost their confidence. Make them aware you noticed their nice jacket, their cute child, their great jewelry etc.

Rule #5 - Stay cool.

Rule #6 - Follow up.

Rule #7 - Follow up again.

These were the rules I set out for myself. In the previous chapters I shared with you all the self- help and business books I read during the time I was in my agoraphobic state. This was, at the time, something that definitively occupied my mind. But never did I think it would affect my future the way that it has. I became strategic with marketing in the simplest forms, by using the simplest techniques.

Branding does not necessarily create sales; it delivers credibility to your name. —**SM**

I set out for myself two things to accomplish:

1. *Do open houses to find clients (the selling part).*
2. *The city must know my name (the branding part).*

With an innovative background being a makeup artist, singer/performer and stager, I began to look at the world I lived in as a large canvas. I started out by creating for myself a relatable slogan that everyone could understand and want as much as I did.

I was a fan of the Jeffersons sitcom growing up, and the theme song was a perfect fit to tell my audience what I' and 'they' should be doing. *"Movin' On Up!"*

I took a risk in spending additional money I really didn't have, on advertising on bus benches and other larger signs along all the main city roads. It took months to get the locations I wanted. I designed the signs so drivers would not miss them and they would stand out strong among all the other captivating ones.

The slogan, the colors, the font, image and my name were all important for drivers to catch it all in the five seconds it took to drive by. I noticed after a few years other agents using similar words, and the city newspaper was infringing on it more than usual for some of their real estate comments.

"Movin' On Up!" (slogan) is a bold statement in the assurance of "onwards and upwards." Who could not relate to that!

In Canada I now hold the trademark for use in real estate.

During the years I struggled through depression and low self-esteem, my life was that of a dying person. It was a life of no hope, other than the optimism in digging deep enough to find that it still existed, and I just needed to find it. Hope!

As you have read in the earlier chapters, hope has driven me to survive through many trials in my life. Although I did not know the end, or where it was taking me I moved forward, without it there was no step to take.

Marketing was an integral new step for me. With all the books I'd read and the lessons I'd learned during the loneliest times of my life, it masterfully threaded itself together like a necklace of gold.

With over seventeen hundred agents competing for business, thinking *"Above the Crowd"* was a mindset I had to adopt. In my second year as an agent, I left the smaller brokerage firm I was working for, and became a RE/MAX real estate agent. By the third year my street bus benches and outdoor recycling box advertising did without a doubt become a solid recognition.

Dave Liniger, founder of RE/MAX, and his wife Gail have achieved a bona-fide and unshakable way to funnel motivation and success to all their broker franchisees, agents, affiliates and clients.

The book, "MY NEXT STEP – *An Extraordinary Journey of Healing and Hope"* is a fantastic read by Dave Liniger. Reading his story put another arrow of strength in my heart to maintain the *I can get through this storm* attitude. The book reveals that "death" knocks on Dave Liniger's door as a sudden ailment befalls him out of nowhere. Although it came by surprise, both he and Gail stayed joined, and fixed on their goal of moving forward. Sickness did not prevail with their demand of a good fight to win! And so they did win that battle! They had climbed many challenging mountains, but going through the trenches was part of that climb. Their tenacity of never giving up in their business helped to maintain the strength in the name they carry today, *"RE/MAX"*! The path they walked and journeyed on brought many downfalls before their true success could arrive. And so with this as their backpack, they were able to endure and fight any new challenge. They were well equipped!

It is true that we see the success of others, and assume their path was easy. We will never know the painful and lonely road they, and many, have had to journey to arrive to meet "Success!"

I once heard someone say, "If you want what I have, you must suffer like I suffered and cry like I've cried." Something that remains true.

Always be willing to fight for your vision, whether it's financial success, overcoming sickness, or mending a relationship that seems impossible to repair. Moving forward in putting strength to your vision will bring you to your next step.

It's not always what we see to "be," but rather things unseen to "become." —SM

With awards given by the Winnipeg Real Estate Board annually, I found myself being in the top 10% a few years in a row, and then in the top 3%. A powerful achievement for someone who once debated taking shock treatments (ECT), unable to work due to chronic depression, agoraphobia, anxieties and panic disorders.

For some of you reading this, you may have made a million in one year instead of four as I did when getting started in my new career. Or possibly you may make an average of $60,000 a year. Some of you reading this may make under $30,000 a year. Last and certainly not least, some of you are where I used to be, on government assistance, emotionally bound, struggling with mental health, fear, and worry.

No matter where we are, there is a place to climb higher, another step to take. A thousand steps are overwhelming, but one is easy, and it all starts with one! —**SM**

This is not to suggest that financial wealth is the only form of prosperity. For me prosperity is having all my children healthy and happy, to have the tools to build whatever I want, to be free from sickness and disease, to live without fear, and lastly to buy what I need. Without it and my desire for it, I've also limited myself to give to anyone else.

37

Silver Linings

On one very cold, stormy winter evening I was stuck doing, or should I say promised to do, an open house for my colleague Viktoria who had gone away on holidays. She had secured this large condo project and needed the display suite to stay open for possible buyers.

The location of this large condo project was smack in the middle of nowhere. For me this was isolation. There were no street lights set up yet, and it was uncomfortable at times being alone when everything was dark outside, and there was little to no traffic inside. A bit eerie, so I kept myself busy on the phone with customer follow-ups. When I was finally done, I thought, "Why don't I call John Wilson and see how he is doing in California?" It was quite a conversation....

John: Hey Suzanne how are you? Long time no hear!

Sue: I'm bored and stuck in this open house and the blizzard is so bad outside that I decided in this down time to call people to whom I owe a phone call.

Breaking

John: Thanks for thinking of me. Things are great out here, other than California is in wildfire season.

Sue: Yes, I've been watching the news.

John: So Grammys are coming up next week. Are you coming?

Sue: Ha! You're kidding right?

John: Not a chance, why don't you come down? This is one Grammy night that will be exceptionally exciting.

Sue: Why would this one be exceptional? Aren't they all?

John: Justin Timberlake is up for a Grammy.

Sue: Great, but I would have expected that, he's Justin Timberlake after all. You're a big fan?

John: Justin Timberlake has put new lyrics over the music of our Sly Slick and Wicked hit song in 1973 called "Sho Nuff." I thought if he's going to win a Grammy for it, I want to be there.

Sue: What is the song called now?

John: "Suit and Tie!"

Sue: "Wow, I love that song, I would not have known the history; great insight!"

"How do you feel about it?" I went on to ask. "Although there have been a few snags that came with this," he said, "the song has been resurrected and I am very proud."

We moved on to talk about one of the songs he helped to produce in the studio with me called "You're Beautiful." This was the music John had sent me from Amir Bayyan, a member of Kool and the Gang. "You're Beautiful" was one of the songs I had shared in an earlier chapter that I wrote lyrics and melody to while on a plane, and recorded it the next day.

"I put the song up on my website," I told John. "I received many compliments on this one. It's got that Kool and the Gang groove and sounds great." "Well I produced it," he said. "Chuckle chuckle!"

"This is true," I responded. "And I am more than happy to pat you on the back for that." (My turn to chuckle.) "However, time is escaping us and I have to close down this open house. It's past 8pm. Have a great time at the Grammys, John, and we will catch up again soon!"

Although Justin Timberlake received a Grammy for the song, John Wilson was awarded the 2014 BMI Pop Award for Best Pop Song in 2014 "Suit and Tie." (He was the "Sly" of Sly, Slick and Wicked Group.)

Onward and busy selling real estate was not something I took for granted. It was my job, even though I fell in love with wanting to be a full-time performer. I had to trust where life was leading me in spite of dreams seemingly being at a distance. I was grateful I had something keeping me productive and prosperous. I wasn't getting any younger. Being a successful performer usually comes with youth, and I was now in my fifties.

Should I kill the dream before the dream kills me? Modifying my vision with other interests was the best thing I could do to keep me positive on a forward road. I wrote a song called *"My Confidence,"* and the chorus read this way:

"Got a war on my hands, not going down, I'll take another round, on my knees I won't bend to the pressure, I'll find what I need and get up again, Got a war on my hands."

If we could find that magic ingredient deep within us to fight that internal "war" we so often struggle with, we would have the confidence to face anything. We would overcome conflicts, adversarial challenges and insecurities. Afraid to face the things that need facing is a confidence diminisher! Something I eventually figured out. I learned that I am the key holder to confidence and I must run to it, not from it.

It's always there, yet it is I who willfully let it out of the gate.

Still dabbling in my music during the busy seasons of real estate, I reminded myself that real estate was my true and bona-fide bread and butter, and music could no longer be in the front lines.

Real Estate was becoming my main focus, and my music had moderately faded for a season. There were many real estate courses, events, and conferences to take in to further my education. And so I soon became bombarded with tackling every quotidian chore, assignment, confabulation, phone call and email related to my business.

I routinely checked my emails first thing after breakfast. I noticed one from the former CBC's Dragon's Den panelist, W. Brett Wilson, also known as Canada's best known entrepreneur, innovative philanthropist, and a member of the order of Canada Advisory Council.

– A formal invitation to the Garden Party –

I had first met Brett at a conference I attended in Las Vegas in my first year of Real Estate. He was the predominant keynote speaker and was undeniably jaw-dropping fabulous. He was flamboyant, yet very becoming in his authentic and personable approach. Certainly not a shy man, but gentle and confident as he earnestly and solemnly took ownership of the stage and the words he spoke. It was a sincere speech on how to find balance in every aspect of one's life. I remember it being so powerful a message that I forgot there were other people in the room. I was centralized and drawn into every word and riveting point he made. The wisdom of his words had quickly tucked away in my heart.

They became life lessons in habitual thinking patterns to bend, sharpen and improve my life. Having balance and keeping check on my habits, good and bad, was not an effortless task for me, as you have read in the earlier chapters.

The Garden Party invitation started with a letter of welcome that included the focus of a Calgary, Alberta non-profit charitable group of Brett Wilson's choice.

His goal was to raise money, lots of money. Generally his annual garden party event raises over $300,000. Each invited guest must bring a check. ("Dig deep," he says.) It's a large yet private party in his elaborate Calgary home estate. The invited guests are family, friends, colleagues and affiliates.

It was an honor to see my name on his invited guest list as it is a limited one, and non-transferable.

Over the last few years I have attended Brett's garden party. It's an old-fashioned back yard party in a lavish garden setting. Indescribably astounding! With Canadian artists like The Sheepdogs Band, Don Amero, and Brett Wilson's favorite Brett Kissel, it's nothing short of being anything but a traditional W. Brett Wilson's unconventional top-notch fundraiser!

Brett Wilson's book - "REDEFINING SUCCESS - *STILL MAKING MISTAKES*" is a magnificent read about understanding the true characteristics of entrepreneurship and philanthropy. After reading it I purchased twelve and gave them away.

A new attitude can take you to new places, and allow you to meet new people. There is something to be said about being at the right place at the right time. It finds you because you've called it out by having a new attitude. A positive approach in every situation can change the wind in your sail and take you to new waters you've never experienced before. Something worth embracing!

38

Tough As Nails

With setbacks of anxiety in my life getting further and further apart, it came to a point where I realized, with the overwhelming amount of people who had confided in me with their struggles of worry, that I wasn't alone in this. "Fake it till you make it" still holds value in certain circumstances.

Yet we all need someone we trust to support and love us through tough times. We also need someone wise and with eyes of vision if they are going to speak into our lives.

We all know someone who loves to hand out advice, yet has no intention of following it themselves. There is also the stereotype, being in one industry and thinking they know about the others and imposing their opinions. I stay away from those people, or maintain my respect for what they do know, not what they don't know. I won't allow them to speak into my situation. Unless the pool maintenance guy knows and understands investments, I won't be asking him for advice about mine any time soon.

---

*A good man giving bad advice is more dangerous than
a nasty man giving bad advice.*
—Conor Cruise O'Brien

Having exercised an about-face attitude, transformation has certainly changed the direction of my life. It has brought positive people in front of me just by a simple mind-altering decision that was ejected from my own thoughts. It changed who I was and what I was about to become.

Here is a quote found in the New Testament that says it all: *Rejoice always!* Two simple words we let escape our thinking. It's finding the good in the bad of every situation, and bringing out the positives, which include thankfulness to the "One" who is greater than you.

When you can find something good in the worst situation, that appears hopeless or even if confusing, you can give credence to "I was blind but now I see!"

---

*New thinking brings new vision, new resources, and a
new perceived reality.* **—SM**

— Back in my real estate world —

Like most realtors® , there are many hours to put in, usually seven days a week. It's challenging to hold a healthy relationship unless you have a partner who supports you 100%. A balance must be strategized that will include your family's time and their opinions. They will and should be a "built in" part of your lifestyle. Family first!

It's very easy to fall off track when you're on a track. No one falls hard when they are on NO track. The distractions will come, as mine did.

With my indomitable courage in moving forward in life, I picked up an intense acumen personality. Serious and thinking about the next step, move or thought was most of my life's moment by moment decisions. It's hard to be humorous or playful when you've faced so many defeating challenges.

It's my life's adjudication to change that every day of my life!

I was introduced to a man who seemed genuine and kind. He had a unique charisma about him that erupted into a charm impossible to resist. As I mentioned in the earlier chapters, if a man had humor, I was easily attracted.

This new man in my life had magnetism, and I was lured in by his softness and how he could make me laugh. When we were alone he gave me the extraordinary "one on one" attention that I longed and hungered for. He found access to my vulnerability.

Alternatively with bringing his insecurities into the relationship, it opened the doors of mine again, bringing out the worst in me. He made alive the person I thought was dead.

He would often fashion his words and actions like art, knowing what to say and what to do at just the right time. When it suited him and not so much when I needed it, and this was the complex part of it. Not to say I was not guilty myself of being insensitive; it's a two way street.

He was passive aggressive in the relationship, and it was hard to understand him. I don't think he was aware that he had brought in baggage from a previous marriage, and this became a dire strait on most of our dates. Neither one of us wanted to fully commit as our insecurities would not allow our guards to drop. It was one of the toughest relationships to pull through. It was the good, the bad and the ugly.

There were, however, many genuine moments of sincere love between us, yet neither one of us would give up the walls we believed needed to remain up in order to protect our hearts from past hurts. And so with enough time, and no one bending, there was nothing left to hold our rope together. The relationship eventually dissolved. Sounds simple but it can also be described as a laceration of the heart.

If both parties are guilty, there is much to consider in change, yet we can only change ourselves and not the other person. A lesson that was learned the hard way for both of us.

So with moving to another RE/MAX office closer to my home, it gave me something new and fresh. Real Estate, real estate, location, location!! The motto of the industry does hold true when you're committed to it. I hit the pavement hard once again, concentrating and focusing on my job. I also consolidated that focus by planning family dinners with my children. I especially relished barbeques on my large back yard deck, then watching my family jump into my swimming pool, laughing and splashing.

They were often busy themselves, and so it was hard to get them all together at the same time. But when I did, I zeroed in on it like a merry event.

With a reconstruction of new changes, commitments and promises to myself, that year I increased my income to approximately fifty percent more than the year prior.

Successful people maintain a positive focus in life, no matter what is going on around them. They stay focused on their past successes rather than their past failures, and on the next action steps they need to take to get them closer to the fulfillment of their goals rather than all the other distractions that life presents to them. **—Jack Canfield**

My new office offered me the perk of being as close as a five minute drive home. It was perfect when working those drudging and tedious long hours.

Having my own office on the second floor away from the main area was a much quieter option. This was going to be my home away from home, so the décor was something of importance to me. A few achievement plaques on the wall to remind me I was my own achiever, and a few positive quotes to prompt my daily thinking. It was only a pocket size 10′ x 12′ office space, but I was certain my visions there would break through impelling and mobilizing energy.

I was ready for it!

Once adjusted in the new office it was afresh "de nouveaux " off to the races of the real estate, real estate, location, location mindset in the life of a hustling realtor®.

Whisking in and out of the office like a speed boat caught on real quick behind the wheel. Always racing to the next appointment without following the laws of the road cost me numerous speeding tickets, which ultimately resulted in temporarily losing my license. Not once but twice. Both times I was suspended for three months. Although I had to get a full-time driver each time, you would think I would have learned my lesson the first time. It wasn't like I was a maniac on the road; I merely went over the speed limit when I thought no one was watching. Yeah right!

Finally I got my license back, and I could start my regular routine at the gym for 6:30am. Just when I thought I was in a "breathe again" momentum, I broke my foot while working out with one of those large thick skipping ropes. As a kid I've tripped on sidewalks, stairs, and rocks, but never a rope.

They gave me an ice pack then practically threw me out the door. Like a snowball's chance, now I was nothing more to them than a probable liability.

Hopping on one foot, I had two choices. Go to the hospital or get ready for my flight to Calgary for my son's wedding, which was the following day. Easy decision, so off to the airport! Once I arrived at the gate, I ran into my oldest son, who could not believe I was hopping on one foot like a raving lunatic, at the airport's security baggage drop off.

"Mom, what the heck happened to your foot?" he asked. I told him the story; he widened his eyes, had a grimaced look on his face, then shook his head to say "Ok, now that we are here I am making arrangements for a wheel chair." You are NOT going to hop through the jet bridge to get to your seat." He commanded like a sergeant in the army. Sheesh!

It was a beautiful wedding, but when it came to me, I was nothing short of a Saturday Night Live comedy act, hopping everywhere in a beautiful elegant dress, with only one fine shoe. And yes, I hopped proudly down the aisle on my son's wedding day, keeping a serious and straight face.

My oldest son and daughter kept in check that I would be in a wheel chair during our weekend mall shopping in Calgary.

They took turns pushing me, often discussing whose turn it was next. I was unquestionably at their mercy. I was sometimes stuck in the mall aisles, as not all stores were suitable for wheel chairs on the chance of knocking something over. With a continual pow-wow between them, surprisingly a communication breakdown still took place. Each child of mine thought the other was in charge of pushing my wheelchair, and I inevitably was forgotten while they were spread out in different stores. "Oops, sorry mom," as they all pointed fingers at each other. It was only about twenty minutes, but I had no idea where everyone went.

Another "Sheesh!!!"

The wedding weekend was over, and I made my way back to Winnipeg, and straight to the emergency room. It wasn't until late in the evening that I received the diagnosis I had already figured out. I had a broken ankle.

After deliberating with the doctors at length and watching everyone else leave with a cast on their foot when I could not was exhausting. "You will never walk normal again unless you let us fix it with a plate and screws." Surgery was what I was hoping to avoid, but the final words of the specialist did convince me to ultimately accept the inevitable.

So like a trooper, I camouflaged my fear and put on a brave mask.

Just as I was wheeled into the surgery room, a very kind nurse grabbed a tissue and gently wiped a tear sliding down my cheek. I wasn't a trooper after all. "You will be fine," she said.

One hour prior while in pre-op I had begun to feel vulnerable and low-spirited. My emotions had suddenly overwhelmed me with the heavy heartedness of feeling alone.

Just before I left for Calgary my ex-boyfriend happened to call, and wanted to meet me for dinner. I had shared with him my dilemma of having to catch a flight for my son's wedding and that I had likely broken my foot. Within the hour he was at my house with an amazing take out dinner, meticulously pampering me.

He insisted on taking me to the airport but I rejected him quickly. "I will take a taxi." "Why?" he asked. "Because we have our own lives now and our paths are different," I replied. This was something he had told me throughout the relationship, and so I reminded him of his own words, even though it was painful. I gave him a kiss, we held each other for a moment, and he left.

Just before they took my mobile phone away in pre-op I had dialed his number a few times, but never pressed the "call" button. He was always off and on with me, and with other women. I just couldn't go back into that space, even though I missed him.

"Whatever are you thinking about?" The nurse nudged me out of my thoughts. "I will be right here," she said. Her timing could not have been more than perfect in reassuring me that I wasn't alone. The pampering and love I longed for in that moment was now substitutive through her.

I stretched my neck to look at her, but my eyes got heavy and began to shut. I allowed the anesthetic to sedate me into a deep and tranquilizing sleep.

39

Recover

Groggy and unsteady, I lazily opened my eyes to see the same comforting smile from the nurse who promised she would be close by. The recovery room was busy, with many other occupied beds lined up end to end. In her soothing voice I heard her say, "Surgery went well and your heart rate is a healthy low. Do you work out?" "I do," I proudly beamed as though she was complimenting me on my figure. (Tongue-in cheek tone)

In a sudden intonation shift, a perplexity came over her facial expression as she paused for a moment to get a blood pressure read. "This is not good," she said as she scrunched her eyes in hopes of getting a better read with a few more attempts. "I just don't understand why your blood pressure shot up so high with such a low heart rate. You could have a stroke at any moment," she boldly asserted. "You won't be leaving the hospital until we can fix this problem. We will be checking your blood pressure every 10 minutes; please stay calm."

With a contemplative thinking of my predicament I heedlessly became emotional, and tears flowed down my cheeks once again However, I remained quiet and still, as instructed by the nurse.

She was the sergeant and I was the soldier. My health and wellbeing were suddenly in her hands, and I chose to submit at this point to any advice she put out there for me. I put my faith in her knowledge of whatever my part was in this. She was my dealer of hope in getting through this without having a stroke.

The French military and political leader Napoleon Bonaparte claimed "A leader is a dealer in hope."

With my foot in a cast and propped on a pillow to prevent swelling, there were no ifs ands or buts choices to make, other than to remain still and think calm thoughts.

With everyone's busy schedule I felt like a nuisance bothering friends and family to take care of me. I went from an independent free-spirited person fully capable of doing everything and anything alone, to needing help with the smallest task.

The morning of the surgery, my friend Vetta picked me up at home, bought me a coffee and dropped me off at the hospital, where an attendant with a wheelchair was there to usher me through. My other friend Tee hung in there with me after the surgery during the high blood pressure crisis.

"Sorry Suzanne" she said, "I'm taking your phone away. This is not the time to catch up on your business. I will answer all of your calls best I can." I made a pledge with her, and promised not to use my phone except to play music from my ITunes library that would be soothing and relaxing. "Agreed," she said. Not only was this acceptable with her but likewise with the patients and nurses in the post-op recovery room. Everyone benefited from the tranquil effects as the music romanced the room.

With most of the day going by and little result in my blood pressure dropping, the doctor suggested an I.V. injection that might help. I believe it was hydralazine, designed to relax and dilate the blood vessels. Again not much change but enough to send me home.

"Please make sure you are not alone for the next 24 hours," the doctor demanded. "Your blood pressure is of priority right now, and you will need to see your family physician as soon as possible so she can prescribe for you a blood pressure medication if it doesn't drop soon. Keep your foot propped up for one to two weeks, and by the way don't expect to work for a while." "Anything else?" I ask facetiously.

My friend Tee was with me most of the post-op time, but her clock was running out to take me home as she had other commitments, and my stay at the hospital was six hours more than expected. My children all had full-time jobs and I tried hard not to inconvenience them, as mothers try not to do. My daughter dropped everything when she received the call that I needed help, and she was there in a flash to get me settled at home.

Every morning became a challenge. It was hard getting out of bed with a propped up foot in a very uncomfortable cast. I couldn't shower, nor could I carry a cup of coffee. With crutches I had no free hands, and with hopping, my coffee would spill. A no-win situation!

Breaking

– When the going gets tough –

The first two weeks was a gargantuan challenge. For breakfast I would start by leaning face on with my kitchen counter where I would raise my foot up on it to rest and to prevent swelling and aching. I would slide one foot across the counter and hop on the other as I reached for bread, the toaster, and to make my morning coffee. Since I couldn't carry anything, I had to eat my breakfast and drink my coffee with one foot up on the counter. If I didn't my foot would swell immediately.

I remember one time sliding my foot cautiously over my L-shaped kitchen countertop. The other foot had to hop along to follow my body in making its way to the utility drawer. With a slight unforeseen imbalance I took a sudden and sharp tumble to the ground.

Back up I went, foot up on the counter, and without notice I had an emotional outburst and abruptly broke out in tears. I lost the capability of functioning normally, and I felt purposeless and alone. It was not a good space to be in, but I couldn't help but to release the desolate and solitary feelings that gushed out of me. It was a solid five minutes of emotional outpouring.

When I finally composed myself, I realized I had to "own the night" as Katy Perry sings in her song "Fireworks."

Do you ever feel already buried deep, six feet under scream
but no one seems to hear a thing. Do you know that there's still a chance
for you

'Cause there's a spark in you.
You just gotta ignite the light and let it shine
Just own the night!
Like the Fourth of July
  (Song Fireworks)

I determined to own the dark cloud of my situation and find my way through it. I put a light on it to shine it!

"Turn your scars into stars" the late Evangelist and motivational speaker Robert H. Schuller would say.

I started the ball rolling by establishing the fact that I needed a full-time driver. I initiated a phone call to find that someone to drive me around the city on all my real estate showings.

"Are you ready, Miss Daisy?" my driver used to say every morning when he picked me up. It was a smile of approbation every time. He was an old friend, or should I say my old neighbor, whom I talked about in the first chapter. He was part of the Lamoix family. He came to my rescue just as I described earlier on. He had now retired from his job and had time on his hands for this type of adventure cruising through the city, running errands and making sure I had a coffee on hand at all times. I was cranky without it. His van became my office, and I couldn't believe the appointments and business I still managed to produce.

His means of transportation was nothing like my slick Mercedes Benz. It was like walking into a hoarder house but in a vehicle. However, I was content to have a driver and so I never once complained about the mess, the rust, or how he rolled his spit around before ejecting it out of his mouth.

Redneck or not, he was there for me to do what I couldn't do for myself, and this was something to be grateful for.

With my foot propped up on the dash board to keep it from swelling, I made myself as comfortable as I could and was able to make all my calls and appointments while being chauffeured around.

Once I arrived to meet my clients to show them the property, he would come around to my side and with a chivalry approach, graciously slide open the van door. Sometimes the junk he collected fell out the moment the door opened.

He was committed and dedicated in helping me balance myself as I tried to get out of the vehicle with the most blunderous oversized cast on my foot. He then acrobatically had to hand-grip clumsy and bulky crutches, holding them, and me, up at the same time.

It was a cumbersome effort going in and coming out of his vehicle, but he was devoted to the challenge of getting me anywhere I needed to be.

Once I was in my office building, which did not have an elevator, I had to get to the second floor. The stairs, located in the receptionist area, made it a little tricky, and embarrassing for anyone watching me.

I would drop my crutches at the bottom of the stairs, do an about face, then sit on each stair gripping with my hands on both sides while pulling my behind up one stair at a time.

Getting to the top was like reaching the summit of a small mountain. I would inevitably need assistance from someone to fetch my crutches, which were still sitting at the bottom. This went on for two weeks.

The same two weeks the doctor demanded I stay home with my foot propped up and to be heavily medicated with pain killers.

Having a metal plate inserted in my foot with several screws was far more invasive than a standard break. Swelling was waiting at the door each time my foot was lowered. Keeping it raised and propped up was a challenge everywhere I went.

———————◗●◖———————

40

Boomerang

Within four to five months I was back in action and wearing what I missed the most, my stilettos! I joined a new fitness center and worked out faithfully every morning at 6am. The workouts were tremendous in helping to lower my blood pressure, which was still problematic.

Many things had slowed down in my life since my foot surgery, my business being one of them. And with that, I determined to pick up the pace once again.

I had been volunteering for several years for our Winnipeg Realtors® annual fundraising event "Gimme Shelter." It was an amazing event to which most of the realtors® on the roster looked forward to buying their tickets to attend, all in support of the Manitoba Real Estate Association Shelter Foundation.

Realtors® giving back to the community was always impressive to me, and from the time I received my Real Estate license, I asked "Where do I sign up?"

My first year, I volunteered my band to play at the event. The entertainment for the evening was comprised of real estate agents and their talents.

The proceeds were and are still in support of Manitoba charities devoted to shelter related causes, and this all through the Manitoba Real Estate Association Shelter Foundation. Each year my involvement became more intensified on the committee, and I eventually became chair.

I was dedicated over the years to always be volunteering somewhere in my community. The Winnipeg Realtors® Association, along with the MREA, seemed fitting while holding a real estate license, and lined up well with my philosophy of helping the less fortunate. It was something I strongly advocated, having experienced the lack of food and shelter myself.

Unfortunately, with many changes going on, and my desperate need to pick up my business to a momentum, it was important to remove myself from volunteering for a short season.

Within a few months I realized that volunteering was truly an important part of my life. It felt as though something was missing, not being involved in a project that was associated with a charity.

I thought of something fresh and new to do. Something that would provide me more time on my hands, and still make me feel like I was contributing to my community. Write checks! There were so many charities that I had never given to, I decided to break free from the others I regularly gave to, and found new non-profit organizations to give to monetarily, as an alternative to volunteering. Time was important to me, and writing a check was a quick fix that allowed me to focus on building my business back up.

It put a colorful change in my world, and it was important for me to learn to dig deep into my pockets.. However, something is better than nothing to give, and it's a measure I've learned that will always come back in a positive way. The only non-profit I will never cease to give to is my local church.

We make a living by what we get, but we make a life by what we give. —**Winston Churchill**

One day I had stopped at a red light, and noticed a non-aggressive panhandler sitting by the roadside. He was holding an old wrinkled cardboard sign written in yellow crayon: *"Can you spare pocket change?"*

He seemed somewhat lethargic and wouldn't even bother walking over to any of the stopped vehicles. Did he really think we would just jump out of our cars and hand him money?

I think not!

Just before the street light turned green, another peddler jumped in the front of my car. He began to wash my windshield with some sort of soggy squeegee that had a broken rubber blade ready to fall off. With only two quick swipes and a sudden knock on my window with his fist, he said loudly, "Please help me; I really need food or money."

"Hmmm…" I thought, "he gave me a choice." Synchronously our eyes locked and I was entranced with an insight of pure and simple empathy. He was either a good actor or displaying his transparency in an authentic sincere cry for help. It was a performance that gripped my heart as I followed those instinctive eyes of genuineness.

His eyes shifted quickly to my passenger side, where a loaf of my favorite spelt bread was exposed outside the grocery bag. Without hesitation I grabbed it and said "Here you go!"

I could see the spring in his step as he walked away while loudly expressing his thank you in an uncanny hoarse and scratchy voice.

Since that day, which was a few years ago now, I've never been short of giving food at any red light stop for any panhandler. It's a quick reach behind my seat in a plastic plant bowl that I found at a thrift store. The container is filled with small bags of dehydrated fruits. Each bag is priced at approximately $1.50. I generally give away three to five bags a day (sometimes more).

I've become so accustomed to it that I feel somewhat guilty when the traffic light is green and I have no alternative than to drive right past them. When this happens I roll my window down and holler "Catch!"

– love makes you generous –

It's the little things that I have found to squeeze in a love language that I relate to. Too often in my life I've had to figure out meals for my children, or needed the community to help me in a time I could not help myself. Life is full of opportunities, and we by-pass or miss them because we are too crammed and occupied in our schedules, or possibly too clouded with worry.

One of the most memorable moments I've had in experiencing deep compassion was when I travelled in New York. I stood after the fall of the World Trade Center, on the site of ground zero sometime after 911. The real Kramer (*a standup comedian who was the inspiration for the character Cosmo Kramer on Seinfeld, who I had met through a musician friend*), arranged with a military person that he and I would enter the grounds.

Although lower Manhattan looked like it had been hit by a nuclear blast, the clean up process was vigilantly in motion with trained and skilled hardworking, dedicated people who loved their city. My heart was heavy with grief and I could not bear the weight of my own feet standing on the same ground that violently stole and swallowed up the lives of innocent and blameless people. I wondered how it was that I could stand so tall, and how long would I stand? The once "tall" that walked every day in this now large and hollow open space had been brought down to a violent and brutal type of holocaust. I could not comprehend as my thoughts rambled and scurried to find the right words. And there were none. We were silent, standing and observing with a common reality that approximately three thousand people died forcibly at the mercy of terrorists. We were silent.

Being Canadian is of no account to me, as we are in a sense all formed and designed to love and to be loved no matter where we originate from. Without our gates we are considered "the human race." Evil will always lurk like a lion seeking out its prey, and so we continue our fundamental action to instinctively lock our doors.

Compassion is a feeling that evolves to the concern for someone other than ourselves. Some will experience it more than others. It's a foundational emotion that I believe can be built on, primarily as we ourselves face our darkest hour. The hard times we face enable us to grow our consciousness with an ability to be sympathetic to the misfortunes of others. It is something I want to learn to do for the rest of my life.

41

Lastly

In writing this book, it has been a painful time in resurfacing heart-wrenching memories. Yet the long hours in front of my computer in reassembling them has proven to be proverbially therapeutic. A fragmented heart still under construction!

In an earlier chapter I shared a true childhood event of running my fingers through a hollow space under the closed and locked bedroom door of my parents. If I could just get my little fingertips to push through the other side I would inevitably feel like I was in the room with them. Afraid of the dark and not being allowed to wake my parents, I lay on that cold floor, quiet as a mouse. I was in fear of them hearing me, because I didn`t want to get spanked. I remember my face scrunched up against the door in an effort to feel close to to my parents. By morning my face and the floor were still wet from the pool of tears I so quietly shed.

– Forgiveness demands change –

I went to visit my eighty four year old mother. She now lives in an assisted living facility that is primarily French speaking.

As she sat across the table from me on June 30th 2017, I shared with her the memory of that little girl, and the purpose of my writing. I told her that I realized forgiveness is my obligation in understanding that her past was not an easy one, and it was all she knew to do, following the footsteps of her father, a strict and severe disciplinarian.

After speaking these words, I saw a clear fluid shadowing her eyes. She began to tear up, as I did with her. She was filled with compassion, something I had longed to see in her eyes. She is a beautiful graceful woman like her mother, the grandmother I loved. This I had failed to see behind the curtain. The pain she had to endure in her own life caused the walls of destruction between us for many years.

I was angry with her until I chose to understand that her behavior was an instinctive pattern from which she did not know how to remedy herself. In getting to know her again I saw a woman who loves.

The best and most beautiful things in the world cannot be seen, nor touched, but are felt in the heart.
—Helen Keller

In moving forward I collect my pearls of experiences that thread themselves in a necklace of treasures.

I still encounter fear while in tight spaces, or when having to take an elevator. But I have travelled a long journey and my performance is spectacular, leaving no evidence that I am tormented on the inside with great anxiety. And so it is when I'm in a social setting with many people, similar to a tight space, I cannot be alone. In a large crowd I cannot be without a companion beside me for a long period of time as I suffer panic inside.

Having to overcome and manage anxieties, panic attacks, agoraphobia, and rejection in my life has given me back my life!

———————◦◦◦———————

Believing in myself has given me the "win" I need, and it can only get better!

Suzanne Mariani

June 30th 2017

2011

news
THE LANCE - Wednesday, October 25, 2000

A message of giving
Winnipeg singer Suzanne Mariani's music video Let's Get Together, shot this past weekend at The Forks, was more than an exercise in choreography. Mariani used the occasion as an appeal for food donations to Winnipeg Harvest. The video will launch her debut CD which will be produced by Chris Burke-Gaffney who helped produce Chantal Kreviazuk and McMaster & James.

Lastly

Day of the 2007 Grammy's

Top: Afternoon with Ike Turner
(Evening He wins best traditional blues album)

Bottom: Lunch with Stony Figueroa & Chris Mancini

2017

2017

Breaking

2017

There are only 24 hours in a day – A lesson to live by each hour/day/year/decade.

Truer Words Were Never Spoken

The less you associate with some people, the more your life will improve.
Any time you tolerate mediocrity in others, it increases your mediocrity.
An important attribute in successful people is their impatience with negative thinking and negative acting people.
As you grow, your associates will change.
Some of your friends will not want you to go on.
They will want you to stay where they are.
Friends that don't help you climb will want you to crawl.
Your friends will stretch your vision or choke your dream.
Those that don't increase you will eventually decrease you.

Consider this:
Never receive counsel from unproductive people.
Never discuss your problems with someone incapable of contributing to the solution, because those who never succeed themselves are always first to tell you how.
Not everyone has a right to speak into your life.
You are certain to get the worst of the bargain when you exchange ideas with the wrong person.
Don't follow anyone who's not going anywhere.
With some people you spend an evening: with others you invest it.

Be careful where you stop to inquire for directions along the road of life.
Wise is the person who fortifies his life with the right friendships.
If you run with wolves, you will learn how to howl. But, if you associate
with eagles, you will learn how to soar to great heights.
A mirror reflects a man's face, but what he is really like is shown by the
kind of friends he chooses.
The simple but true fact of life is that you become like those with whom
you closely associate - for the good and the bad.

Note: Be not mistaken.

This is applicable to family as well as friends.
Yes...do love, appreciate and be thankful for your family, for they will
always be your family no matter what.
Just know that they are human first and though they are family to you,
they may be a friend to someone else and will fit somewhere in the criteria
above.

In Prosperity Our Friends Know Us.
In Adversity We Know Our Friends.

Never make someone a priority when you are only an option for them.

If you are going to achieve excellence in big things, you develop the habit
in little matters. Excellence is not an exception, it is a prevailing attitude.
                                                              —Colin Power

And To GOD I say – Because you are supreme and matchless, protect the investment of every infallible and indubitable prayer brought to you.

—*Suzanne Mariani*

CPSIA information can be obtained
at www.ICGtesting.com
Printed in the USA
LVOW03s0254061017
551366LV00002B/2/P